THOMAS CH

Selected Poems

Edited with an introduction by
GREVEL LINDOP

Fyfield*Books*

CARCANET

First published in Great Britain in 1972 by
Carcanet Press Limited
Alliance House
Cross Street
Manchester M2 7AQ

This impression 2003

A CIP catalogue record for this book is available from the British Library
ISBN 1 85754 692 X

The publisher acknowledges financial assistance from
the Arts Council of England

Printed and bound in England by SRP Ltd, Exeter

SELECTED POEMS

THOMAS CHATTERTON was born in Bristol in 1752. His father, a schoolmaster, died shortly after his birth and his mother lived by running a school and taking in sewing. An unhappy, withdrawn child who had been expelled from school, Chatterton taught himself to write and draw from old manuscripts that he had found his mother tearing up as waste paper. In 1760 he was sent to a Bristol charity school intended to prepare poor children for employment or apprenticeship. At this time he first began to write 'medieval' poetry. In 1767 Chatterton was apprenticed to John Lambert, a Bristol attorney, and began to widen his circle of readers, forging medieval manuscripts to sell to local patrons. Encouraged by his success, he forced Lambert to release him from his apprenticeship on 14 April 1770, and left Bristol for London a few weeks later. He managed to write and publish his work for the first few months, but payments were too small and irregular for him to live on. He moved to cheaper lodgings, and too proud to admit failure and accept help from relatives, killed himself on 24 August 1770 by drinking arsenic.

GREVEL LINDOP was born in Liverpool (UK) in 1948 and educated at Oxford. He lives in Manchester, where he was Professor of Romantic Studies and British Academy Research Reader at Manchester University. His *Selected Poems* were published in 2000. Grevel Lindop's prose publications include *The Opium-Eater: A Life of Thomas De Quincey* (1981), *A Literary Guide to the Lake District* (1993), and *The Path and the Palace: Reflections on the Nature of Poetry* (1997). His editorial work includes the Robert Graves centenary edition of *The White Goddess*, and *The Works of Thomas De Quincey* (21 volumes, in progress).

FyfieldBooks aim to make available some of the great classics of British and European literature in clear, affordable formats, and to restore often neglected writers to their place in literary tradition.

FyfieldBooks take their name from the Fyfield elm in Matthew Arnold's 'Scholar Gypsy' and 'Thyrsis'. The tree stood not far from the village where the series was originally devised in 1971.

> *Roam on! The light we sought is shining still.*
> *Dost thou ask proof? Our tree yet crowns the hill,*
> *Our Scholar travels yet the loved hill-side*

from 'Thyrsis'

CONTENTS

PREFACE

My debts to the chief Chatterton scholars will be obvious to the reader. My introduction and notes rest heavily upon Skeat's edition of Chatterton's *Poetical Works* (London, 1875), which I have also used as the basis for the text of the acknowledged poems. E. H. W. Meyerstein's *Life of Thomas Chatterton* (London, 1930) was, of course, invaluable. Donald S. Taylor's edition of Chatterton's *Complete Works* (Oxford, 1971), which appeared whilst I was at work on this selection, provided much-needed factual information and a text for the Rowley poems against which I was able to check my own inadequate text. Taylor's splendid volumes provide a fitting monument for Chatterton, and it is good to be able unreservedly to recommend them to readers who wish to know more of Chatterton's work.

I am grateful to the staff of the English Faculty Library, Oxford, for their help in checking some elusive facts; to Rachel Laird for constant encouragement, and advice on the organisation of the book; and to Michael Schmidt for confirming my belief that the job was worth doing.

The selection is dedicated, as I think it could only be, to the memory of Thomas Chatterton.

Manchester   October 21, 1971   GREVEL LINDOP

INTRODUCTION

I THE POET

Thomas Chatterton was born in Bristol on November 20, 1752. His father, who died shortly before the poet's birth, had been a schoolmaster and sub-chanter at the Church of St. Mary Redcliff; his mother, who was then twenty-one years old, lived by keeping a 'dame-school' and taking in sewing.

These were not auspicious beginnings; and indeed, throughout his early childhood Chatterton showed no signs of talent. He was regarded as little better than an idiot until he was about six and a half years old, because he would learn nothing, refused to play with other children, and spent most of his time brooding in silence. He was expelled from his first school as a dullard.

When all allowance has been made for partiality on the part of those who knew Chatterton and supplied anecdotes to the biographers in the years after his death, it still appears that he underwent a considerable transformation in his seventh year. The story goes that one day he found his mother tearing up for waste paper some old music folios which had been brought home from the church some years previously by his father for use as sewing-patterns, bookbindings and the like. According to his mother, Thomas 'fell in love' with the illuminated capitals and, his interest once aroused, his mother soon taught him to read with the aid of the manuscript. If the story can be trusted, it illustrates vividly both Chatterton's instinctive delight in medieval art and the philistinism of his surroundings.

At all events, his reading progressed from the old folios to a black-letter Bible (his sister remarked many years later, in an odd phrase that has the authentic ring of Chatterton's splendid obstinacy, that 'he always objected to read in a small book') and thence to any books he could obtain. At this period he is said to have been intensely proud, and given to telling small lies to save himself inconvenience. He spent a great deal of his time locked in the attic, where he would write and draw for hours together.

In August 1760 he began attending Colston's Hospital, a Bristol charity-school which formed probably the worst intellectual environment he could have had. Colston's was virtually an elementary business-school which aimed to teach its pupils the bare minimum required to get them an apprenticeship or place as a junior clerk. It had been founded in 1708 by Edward Colston, a bachelor business-man whose often-repeated comment on his single state had been 'Every helpless widow is my wife, and distressed orphans my children'. This Dickensian personage had left behind him a school run like a prison, where the pupils were tonsured like monks and suspected leanings towards religious non-conformity were punishable by expulsion.

Chatterton's behaviour there seems to have alternated between delinquency and sullenness. His only recorded comment on the school was that 'he could not learn so much at school as he could at home, for they had not books enough there'. His mother had done her best for him, but the school proved to be the first of a series of disastrously stultifying milieux which certainly contributed to Chatterton's tragedy.

When he was ten, he began to write poetry. At first he produced religious verses, but he soon developed a satirical vein : the poem *Apostate Will,* included in this selection, was written when he was eleven. At about this time also he made friends with Thomas Phillips, a pupil-teacher at the school who also wrote poetry. Phillips, several years Chatterton's senior, encouraged him; but it seems clear that the younger boy was greatly superior to the elder in intelligence and often became impatient with him.

It is through Phillips that we catch our first glimpse of Chatterton as literary forger, for it seems that in 1764, before he was twelve, Chatterton one day presented Phillips with a 'medieval' poem, written on parchment with dull ink and in barely legible calligraphy. The parchment was singed, and cut about the edges.

8

Apparently Phillips accepted the poem as a medieval manuscript, but lost interest in it after some unsuccessful attempts to read it and to clarify the letters by retracing them with his own pen. Chatterton claimed to have 'found' the parchment, and presumably had no motive in making it other than to fool his dull friend. But it was a dangerous precedent.

In 1767, when he was nearly fifteen, Chatterton left school and was apprenticed to John Lambert, an attorney. It was his first step into the business world, an environment which he found almost as oppressive as Colston's Hospital.

Bristol at this time was an overcrowded, bustling industrial city crammed into a set of streets and buildings which had changed little since the middle ages. It was, in fact, one of the places where the modern world was coming into existence. The middle classes of Bristol were well known for their ostentatious materialism and cultural obtuseness, and the men with whom Chatterton came into contact through his work at Lambert's, and whom he seems to have tried to use as patrons, were entirely incapable of appreciating his gifts.

The first of this sorry procession was Henry Burgum, partner in the firm of 'Burgum and Catcott, Pewterers and Worm- [i.e. screw-] Makers'. Burgum was a pleasant enough man, but uneducated and socially ambitious, attempting to conceal his plebeian manners and speech under an imperfect veneer of gentility. He befriended Chatterton, probably with some condescension, and so became his second dupe. Chatterton mentioned to Burgum one day that he had discovered an old pedigree showing the noble descent and heraldic achievements of Burgum's family. He soon produced the document, artificially 'aged', and (probably to Chatterton's surprise) Burgum was entirely taken in. The hoax was discovered only when Burgum sent the pedigree to the Royal College of Heralds for authentication.

Meanwhile, Chatterton was not proving a satisfactory apprentice. Set to the drudgery of copying legal precedents, he whiled

9

away the time in drawing and writing poetry. He still read enormously. He was sulky and sardonic, and began to associate in his spare time with a group of young apprentices who, like him, were bored by their work and did their best to enliven the evenings with drinking and chasing girls. Moreover, Chatterton's employer was particularly disturbed on coming home late one night to find him busily attempting to raise spirits with the help of a book of magical incantations.

His literary work went ahead quickly. In 1768 a local magazine accepted from him a 'medieval' document relating to a matter of local history. And before long he was selling to George Catcott, Burgum's partner, a series of 'medieval' poems and documents, which he claimed to have found amongst old papers in the Church of St. Mary Redcliff. Catcott was a tempting target. He was extremely pompous and fancied himself as a bibliophile. One can imagine Chatterton's delight at making an ass of him; also, perhaps, his bitterness at Catcott's regarding the poems solely as curios, with no regard for them as literature. Among the poems he gave to Catcott was the manuscript of his masterpiece, *Ælla*.

Chatterton developed a similar relationship with the local surgeon and amateur historian, William Barrett. But here one suspects a kind of double-bluff. Barrett was a cultured and rather cynical man. He was writing a *History of Bristol,* and the 'documents' supplied to him by Chatterton provided new and exciting 'evidence' about the history of the city. It seems probable that Barrett saw through the forgeries (and indeed he slyly hinted as much to Chatterton) but felt that their contents would improve his history so much (even at the expense of truth) that he was willing to turn a blind eye to the fraud, and hope that it would never be discovered.

At this point it becomes necessary to face the question, why did Chatterton turn forger? Why was he not content to be a poet? It must be admitted, first of all, that there was a certain basic perver-

10

sity about his character. He felt something of a grudge towards society, and especially towards figures of authority. He was naturally sensitive and suspicious. He was extraordinarily intelligent, perhaps even a genius, and yet he was placed in a series of environments which offered little understanding or encouragement. In the early forgeries, one can almost see a tendency to test the various dupes, to find out how much they would swallow. And what these experiments revealed was that the ignorance of the Bristolian worthies was boundless. Most galling of all, perhaps, was the fact that when, on a few well-documented occasions, Chatterton admitted that he had written the poems, no-one would believe him. He was not regarded as sufficiently intelligent. This above all must have confirmed him in his resolution to play merely the discoverer and editor of a medieval poet, and not to claim the authorship for himself.

A second line of explanation is purely historical. Chatterton is generally regarded as the first Romantic poet in English. But there had been signs of an approaching end to the rule of Common Sense, Reason and neo-Classical decorum over English poetry. In 1760 James MacPherson had published *Fragments of Poetry Translated from the Gaelic and Erse Languages*; in 1764 Horace Walpole had published his Gothic novel *The Castle of Otranto,* which he claimed was a translation from an old Italian manuscript. Both works were in a sense forgeries. MacPherson had composed the *Fragments* himself; Walpole had written *Otranto.* The obvious explanation for the concealment of authorship in both cases was that the authors were producing works of such a new kind that they were unable to predict the public reaction, and wanted to guard against the possible ridicule of the formidable eighteenth-century critics. By claiming to have revived ancient works they were also dramatically affirming their links with the pre-Renaissance periods whose sensibilities they believed they were restoring to the world.

There can be no doubt that these factors were important to

11

Chatterton. A poem which would be accepted and perhaps sincerely acclaimed as a specimen of medieval verse would be cruelly ridiculed as the work of a living poet; or so he probably assumed. And with some of the disinterest of the true artist, Chatterton sacrificed his own fame and attributed most of the poems he wrote in 1768 and 1769, many of which touch on greatness, to a fictitious Bristolian priest of the fifteenth century, Sir Thomas Rowley.

Unfortunately Chatterton, herald of the new poetic era, still clung to some of the habits of the old. He seems to have wanted a patron; and in his innocence, it occurred to him that Walpole, author of *Otranto*, was the very man.

Walpole had just published a volume of art history, *Anecdotes of Painting*, and Chatterton followed the cue, sending Walpole a 'transcript' of a work on *The Ryse of Peyncteynge yn Englande*, supposed to be the work of Rowley, together with some samples of Rowley's poetry. Walpole was taken in and wrote an enthusiastic reply. But now Chatterton pushed his luck too far: he sent Walpole more poems, and explained that he desired to give his life to literature and scholarship but lacked the means to do so. Walpole became suspicious, some bad-tempered correspondence followed, and eventually the manuscripts were returned to Chatterton with a curt letter. Walpole has been blamed for his treatment of the poet, but he could scarcely have deduced from the fragments he received what kind of youth he was dealing with. And one may suspect that he was annoyed at having initially been deceived, especially as he was himself the author of the pseudo-antique *Otranto*. Walpole was a busy and decisive man, Chatterton a comparative innocent; and the rest was inevitable.

However, those poems which Chatterton acknowledged as his own (the more conventional satires, elegies and so on) had had some success in Bristol, and had begun to appear in the *Town and Country Magazine* in London. In 1769 Chatterton decided that he must leave the attorney's office and turn professional. But he was still bound by his indentures to Lambert, and there was no

12

easy way to obtain release. He became increasingly depressed and frequently talked of suicide. His religious beliefs had partly fallen away and after one suicide-threat Lambert called in the worldly-wise Barrett, as the only person who could command Chatterton's respect, to give the young man a serious lecture on the wickedness of self-destruction.

But Chatterton won. On April 14, 1770 Lambert found on his desk Chatterton's 'Last Will and Testament', a document so characteristic that I give part of it in Appendix B. The threat that he would be dead by eight o'clock the following evening was too much for Lambert to pass over. He cancelled Chatterton's indentures.

Free at last, Chatterton, now seventeen, set out for London at the end of April. In his pocket he carried a document which, although written half in jest, establishes even better than the 'Will' his claim to be a forerunner of Byron :

The Articles of the Belief of Me Thomas Chatterton

That God being incomprehensible: it is not required of us to know the mysterys of the Trinity &c. &c. &c. &c.

That it matters not whether a Man is a Pagan Turk Jew or Christian if he acts according to the religion he professes

That if a man leads a good moral Life he is a Christian

That the Stage is the best School of Morality

and

The Church of Rome (some Tricks of Priestcraft excepted) is certainly the true Church

T. Chatterton

He lodged at first with relatives in Shoreditch. He was as proud as ever, and rebuked his hostess for calling him 'Cousin Tommy' on the grounds that it was no fitting name for a poet. He visited the editors of several magazines and seems to have written and published a great deal of satirical verse and prose in the first few months. But payments were small and irregular and the work exhausting. Although he continued to write home in the most cheerful terms, and even went hungry to send his mother and sister a box of presents as a token of his prosperity, the struggle of writing for his bread soon became a hopeless one. In June he moved to cheaper lodgings in Brook Street, Holborn, where he need not be seen in his exhaustion and poverty by anyone who knew him. He was entirely alone, and could not bring himself to return to Bristol a failure. He was half-starved, and there is evidence to suggest that his sufferings were aggravated by a dose of gonorrhoea. On August 24, 1770, proud to the end, he refused his compassionate landlady's offer of an evening meal and locked himself into his room. There he poisoned himself by drinking arsenic in water. It seems likely (and one hopes it is true) that he first chewed opium to deaden the pain caused by the poison.

The room was broken open the next day. Chatterton's body lay on the bed, severely convulsed. The floor was littered with fragments of manuscript. The inquest, the records of which have been lost, presumably returned the plain verdict of suicide, so that Chatterton's body was buried in an unmarked grave near Shoe-Lane Workhouse. Two centuries of demolition and new building have obliterated the burial ground, and it is now impossible even approximately to locate the grave.

II THE POETRY

Chatterton's poems fall quite naturally into two groups: those poems written in the conventional style of the period and which he acknowledged as his own; and those written in an elaborately 'antique' manner, most of which were attributed to the fictitious poet-priest Sir Thomas Rowley.

The acknowledged poems are varied in subject-matter and variable in quality. From the age of eleven Chatterton wrote satirical verse: one of his earliest such pieces, *Apostate Will*, is included in this selection. His models were Pope, Swift, Gay and their

14

lesser followers, but from an almost incredibly early age he had great facility in verse and many of the satires have a quirky intelligence and vigorous, boyish humour which make them quite distinctive. It is to exemplify these qualities that I have chosen *Apostate Will*, and the discursive satires *The Defence, The Art of Puffing* and the section beginning 'Say, Baker!' from *Journal 6th*. The last piece in particular, written when Chatterton was sixteen, illustrates the poet's intelligent and independent outlook : despite the jocular tone, it is fundamentally a serious and urbane definition of two opposing approaches to love. Behind the humorous panegyric on the Rake one senses a cheerfully mature attitude to sexual relations. Chatterton modestly speaks as a mere onlooker, but his attitude is an appealing one.

The more earnest discursive poems are less successful : the passionate but incomplete *To Horace Walpole* is conventional in diction and undisciplined in feeling, although Chatterton's prose note adds a touch of irresistible bathos; and *On the Immortality of the Soul* is interesting for what it tells us about Chatterton's advanced but somewhat confused religious beliefs. Chatterton was a neat hand at an elegy, and I include both a serious and a humorous example of his work in the genre. The debt to Gray is obvious, but Chatterton adds extravagant touches which can fairly be called Romantic. It is interesting that here as elsewhere Chatterton was caught between two kinds of sensibility, for he 'expunged' from the *Elegy on Phillips* a whole stanza of colourful landscape-painting (lines 101-104) 'as too flowry for grief'. Clearly, the poet Chatterton was Romantic, whilst the critic in him remained Augustan. The mock-elegy *February* is really a city-eclogue owing a good deal to Gay's *Trivia* (it may be significant that in line 3 Chatterton wrote *Gay* by mistake for *Gray*) but it pleasantly displays the poet's boisterous humour and his antipathy to Bristol's civic dignitaries. Both poems also exemplify his considerable gift for presenting a scene and a time of day. Delightful passages describing a morning or an evening, a change in the seasons or

15

in the weather, appear consistently throughout both the acknow-ledged and the Rowley poems, and form perhaps the most obvious of his many similarities to Keats.

I have included also the poem *To Miss Hoyland,* because it shows Chatterton's sense of humour breaking in and turning a conven-tionally straight-faced poem into knock-about satire—surely an irresistible love-poem, had Chatterton not been acting as proxy for a friend.

The bulk of the other acknowledged poems consists of thoroughly conventional satire, often ill-tempered and pretentious and some-times incoherent. It is doubtful whether anyone could now derive much pleasure from *The Consuliad* or *Kew Gardens.* At best they testify only to Chatterton's skill as a versifier and ape of contemporary fashion.

I have omitted also the *African Eclogues,* a curious set of poems blending pastoral convention with exotic 'African' descrip-tive passages. Rimbaud has been mentioned in this connection, but the comparison is not a serious one and modern readers, I think, find little pleasure in them. Their importance to literary history does not seem to me to warrant their inclusion in a neces-sarily small selection.

The Rowley poems, so called for convenience although not all were attributed to Rowley, constitute the real basis of Chatterton's fame. The technicalities of their language will be discussed below, so I confine myself here to general matters of their style and content.

The claim that in these poems we have the first Romantic poetry is not a frivolous one. They are Romantic in the decorative rich-ness of their imagery, their keen celebration of human emotion and their delight in the mysterious. They are also characteristic of the first phase of the 'Romantic Revival' in their harking back to an age when scientific knowledge, 'common sense' and capitalism were not dominant factors in social and intellectual life.

Chatterton creates in these poems an idealised vision of medieval

16

Bristol. His self-education was probably a crucial factor in the process, for he picked out for reading works which were not the usual staple of eighteenth-century education : obscure works on history, heraldry and magic; the poetry of Chaucer, as well as of Spenser and Shakespeare. Perhaps the most important detail is that he knew virtually nothing of the classics.

The Rowley poems were written in a comparatively short space of time, principally in 1768 and 1769. They include lyrics, satires, eclogues, narrative verse and poetic drama. All are characterised by an extraordinary richness of imagery, and most by great technical dexterity. I have chosen (over-indulgently, perhaps) only those poems or passages which I thought likely to give the reader fairly immediate pleasure, but even so the quality of the material has made selection difficult. My main hope is that the small sample displayed in this volume will lead readers to search the treasury itself, since the whole of Chatterton's work is now available in Donald S. Taylor's excellent two-volume edition.

Ælla, in part at least, could not be omitted. This play, set in pre-Conquest England, is certainly unperformable; but it must surely be one of the greatest 'closet-dramas' in English. The complicated ten-line stanza is maintained with amazing skill, hindering neither action nor dialogue but adding a sustained and varied music which will be found in few other rimed plays. The construction of the piece is virtually flawless, and it is hard not to agree with Meyerstein that Chatterton was a natural dramatist as Keats, for example, was not.

Ælla contains also some of Chatterton's best lyrics, including the famous *Roundelay* which is probably his best-known poem and which provides a direct link with Keats, who, according to Bailey, was wont to 'recite, or *chant,* in his peculiar manner', the stanza beginning 'Com with acorne coppe and thorne . . .' (lines 1010-1016). 'The first line to his ear possessed the great charm', Bailey adds.

The affinity felt by Keats for Chatterton has been discussed by the biographers of both poets, and they undoubtedly share certain qualities of perception. A single couplet from *Ælla* (the context of these lines, sadly, does not quite merit inclusion in this short selection) will suffice without further comment to illustrate the point :

The shepster mayden, dyghtynge her arraie,
Scante sees her vysage in the wavie glasse . . . (lines 1250-1)

I have tried to include samples of all the Rowleian moods. At times the poems become repetitious : for this reason I have chosen only a short sample of *The Parlyamente of Sprites.* In view of its similarities to *Ælla* and its boyish clumsiness I have omitted *The Battle of Hastings.* Chatterton made two attempts at a poetic account of the battle, but since he persisted in treating it as a series of single combats the poems become intolerably repetitive and shapeless.

Form, however, is one of the great virtues of several shorter Rowleian pieces, and in this they differ from even the best of the acknowledged poems. I have therefore included entire *An Excelente Ballade of Charitie, The Gouler's Requiem, The Worlde* and the best of the *Eclogues.* I very much hope that readers will want to read more of the poems than I can include, but they must be warned that short as it is this selection contains practically all those poems which can be wholeheartedly praised for their construction, as distinct from style or matter.

To vary the selection I add three purely comic poems, one at least a model of compactness. As an introduction to the Rowleian style, I cannot do better than recommend *The Broder of Orderys Blacke.*

III THE TECHNICALITIES OF ROWLEY

What Chatterton sought in the style of the Rowley poems was the appearance of antiquity. He aimed at this, probably, not merely as a means of deception, but also as a way of invoking the mysterious charm of the past which was psychologically necessary for the composition of his best work.

To what extent he 'translated' the poems from modern to Rowleian English is not clear. But from a strictly technical point of view it is simplest to approach the eccentricities of the Rowleian style as if they were added and worked into a pre-existing poem.

Although the dates he claimed for them varied widely, Chatterton was probably trying to give the poems a general appearance similar to that of Chaucer's works as they appeared in the rather imperfect editions of the day. He used three principal methods to achieve this: the alteration of spelling, the introduction of archaisms both genuine and spurious, and the disruption of grammar.

The changes in spelling are simple and even consistent. Any word that can conveniently take a terminal *e* does so. Thus *soul* becomes *soule*. Consonants are often doubled: *royal* becomes *royalle*; *y* and *i* are interchangeable, so that *fire* becomes *fyre* and (more confusingly) *my* becomes *mie*. This is all simple enough, but indiscriminate application of these principles can produce such monstrosities as *telleynge* (telling) and *albeytte* (albeit). Chatterton also introduces silent consonants where they seem appropriate, so that (e.g.) *soul* is often *soughle*. Some consonant-groups are repeatedly altered: *sh* becomes *sch* and *th, dh*. Clearly Chatterton had picked up the notion that middle-English spelling was laborious and somewhat grotesque, and he reproduces these characteristics with enthusiasm.

Rowley's vocabulary is a more complicated matter. Chatterton drew most of his archaisms from dictionaries or glossaries borrowed from his more affluent friends or from the local circulating library. They included the dictionaries of Skinner, Kersey and Nathaniel Bailey, and the glossary to Speght's edition of Chaucer. From these he lifted a large number of archaisms, including a good many which were disfigured by misprints, simple errors of scholar-

19

ship or (in the case of the Chaucer) dubious textual readings. It is largely these errors that enable us to trace back so many of Chatterton's 'archaisms' to their precise sources. For example, Chatterton more than once uses a dialect-word *heck* to mean *rock*. He derived the word from Kersey's dictionary, unaware that Kersey had misprinted the definition, which should have read not *rock* but *rack*. Again, he uses *cherisaunei* to mean *comfort*. This is miscopied from Bailey's *cherisaunie*, which in turn is a misprint for the genuine Chaucerian *cherisaunce*.

Other errors are assumed to have arisen from Chatterton's habit of listing old words in a notebook. He borrowed, probably from Kersey's dictionary, the participle *lissed*, meaning *bounded* or *encircled*. Having written the words together thus, '*Lissed, bounded*', Chatterton later misunderstood '*Bounded*', assuming it to mean *leaped about*; and this is how he uses it in the poems. Such errors are common, and some of the more interesting ones are mentioned in the notes to this selection. When we take into account also the numerous words which Chatterton coined himself, it becomes easy to accept Skeat's estimate that only about seven per cent of the Rowleian archaisms are authentic and correctly used.

Rowleian grammar is largely a matter of inconsistency in small details. Again, Chatterton is probably imitating the unreliable eighteenth-century editions of Chaucer when he gives us a plural subject with a singular verb, or *vice versa*. At times articles or auxiliaries are omitted, and word order oddly disrupted. It must be remembered that for the common reader of Chatterton's day, non-classical antiquity meant essentially grotesqueness of form and obscurity of meaning, and these were the characteristics he reproduced. His genius is apparent in the fact that such a process should have led to a more vigorous and harmonious verse than he could otherwise have achieved.

IV CHATTERTON'S REPUTATION

Strange as it may seem in view of the facts reviewed above, the earliest criticism of Chatterton was bedevilled by the question of whether or not the Rowley poems were genuine. The 'Rowley Controversy' was at its height at the end of the eighteenth century, but continued well into the nineteenth. The controversy seems to have attracted people of the same type as were later to take up the Baconian theory of the authorship of Shakespeare's plays. There was not a shred of evidence on the side of the 'Rowleians', as those critics became known who claimed genuine medieval authorship for the poems; and as in the case of Baconians, their chief argument was that an ill-educated poet could scarcely have written such fine poetry. As scholarly evidence was assembled by such expert etymologists and textual critics as Tyrwhitt and Skeat, showing that Rowley's language could be explained entirely with reference to a limited number of dictionaries and glossaries to which Chatterton was known to have had access, the Rowleians took refuge in the theory that Chatterton had *seen* some old poems and then adapted them, falsifying the texts through haste and ignorance. This view persisted into the twentieth century, and for all I know may still claim a few adherents. But all the evidence is against it.

From the beginning of the nineteenth century, however, the controversy dropped into the background and Chatterton's reputation as a poet grew. His work became widely known, and was seized upon with particular eagerness by his fellow-poets. Both Keats and Shelley would certainly have written quite differently without his example; Coleridge worked on his *Monody on the Death of Chatterton* almost throughout his writing life, and experimented with Rowleian metres in *Christabel*; and Wordsworth wrote the tribute through which Chatterton's name is probably best-known today, hailing him as,

21

The marvellous boy,
The sleepless soul that perished in his pride . . .
                    (*Resolution and Independence,* 43-4)

In a sense, simply by virtue of his historical position Chatterton's work contains in essence the whole of Romanticism. Similarities to Keats and Shelley, Wordsworth and Coleridge are clear enough. But consider these lines :

The clock strikes eight; the taper dully shines;
Farewell, my Muse, nor think of further lines:
Nine leaves, and in two hours, or something odd,
Shut up the book; it is enough by God!
                    (*Conversation,* 47-50)

In such passages we can already hear the voice of Byron and, at a further remove, of Heine and Pushkin.

Predictably, then, the poets stayed faithful to Chatterton; the public did not. By mid-century Chatterton was already something of a 'poet's poet'. His work retained its technical interest, and yielded as much as ever to careful readers. But for the public he was out of date : his advances had been followed up by other poets; and poets, moreover, who did not lard their poems with hard words. A lack of clearly-printed and simply-edited texts helped to damage his reputation further. The Chatterton legend survived, but by the present century the poems had come to seem mere stylistic curiosities. Even E. H. W. Meyerstein's *Life* (1930) does not seem to have rescued his reputation.

Now, however, a little over two centuries after his death, we are perhaps able once more to see Chatterton in the proper perspective. The poetry of the eighteenth century has returned to favour, and without a serious corresponding fall in the 'stock' of the Romantics; so that we are able to approach Chatterton sympathetically through both his Augustan predecessors and his Romantic successors. Modern readers are willing to put some work into their reading of poetry, and an Englishman who can comfortably read, say, MacDiarmid will not find Chatterton a serious problem. The Rowleian dialect is quickly learned, and it yields ample rewards.

V THE TEXT AND EDITORIAL MATTER

My criteria for selection are probably apparent by now. I have tried to show Chatterton's range and qualities, and to reveal something of his curious personality, perplexing, forbidding and endearing as it is. My first priority always has been the profit of the reader.

In the text, I have aimed at readability. When one examines many previous editions and selections, one begins to wonder whether their intention was to discourage the reading of the poet. The text is often speckled with numerals or asterisks or both, a few of them Chatterton's own but most editorial. Some typographers, perhaps feeling that the Rowley poems had an unduly modern appearance, have tried to improve matters by using italic or gothic type, or the long S.

I have eschewed such mannerisms, giving the text of both acknowledged and Rowley poems plain. Obscure words in the Rowley poems are glossed at the foot of the page, identified by line numbers; the Rowleian being in italics, the gloss in roman type. Inevitably I shall have glossed too many words for some readers, too few for others; but unless I had followed Skeat in modernising and thereby rewriting the poems so far as rime and meter permitted, some choice had to be made. It should be remembered that the glosses are merely local: they explain a word in a single context only, and on the next page a different shade of meaning may require a different explanation. Where a common Rowleyism is repeated several times in a single poem, I do not gloss it all the way through.

This method will, I hope, permit the reader to treat the poems as poems and take or leave the glosses at will.

23

The text itself follows Skeat's in the case of the acknowledged poems, with a few corrections from Taylor's edition, which appeared whilst I was at work on this selection. In the case of the Rowley poems I follow Taylor's text. In either case, any textual errors are certainly my own.

I have repunctuated poems when I felt that Chatterton's hasty punctuation did not help the reader, and in the acknowledged poems I have regularised spelling, use of italics and elisions.

In several cases I have taken a number of extracts from a single poem. I have tried to select these so that they still read as one poem, the points at which cuts appear marked by a row of asterisks. I have numbered the lines as for the full poem, so that a reader can estimate the size of the gaps and if he wishes supply them from Taylor's edition.

The notes give the minimum amount of information and interpretation I felt to be necessary to a satisfactory reading of the poems. I include a few notes from Skeat's edition, most of which mingle their instruction with a dry humour I was loath to omit.

The appendices give two documents which I thought might be of interest to readers. I can justify the inclusion of the forged 'Last Verses' only on the grounds that they are well-known, and that they give us a vivid picture of how a subsequent generation (the lines were probably written in or shortly before 1857) liked to see Chatterton. At any rate, the fact that the verses are a forgery in no way diminishes their fitness as a memorial tribute. Forgery may not be the sincerest form of flattery, but it is at least a gesture of faith in the durability of a reputation.

Acknowledged Poems

Apostate Will

In days of old, when *Wesley's* power
Gather'd new strength by ev'ry hour;
Apostate Will, just sunk in trade,
Resolv'd his bargain should be made;
Then straight to *Wesley* he repairs,   5
And puts on grave and solemn airs,
Then thus the pious man address'd :
" Good sir, I think your doctrine best;
Your servant will a *Wesley* be,
Therefore the principles teach me."   10
The preacher then instructions gave,
How he in this world should behave :
He hears, assents, and gives a nod,
Says ev'ry word's the word of God,
Then lifting his dissembling eyes,   15
" How blessed is the sect !" he cries;
" Nor *Bingham, Young,* nor *Stillingfleet*
Shall make me from this sect retreat."
He then his circumstance declar'd,
How hardly with him matters far'd,   20
Begg'd him next morning for to make
A small collection for his sake.
The preacher said, " Do not repine,
The whole collection shall be thine."
With looks demure and cringing bows,   25
About his business straight he goes.
His outward acts were grave and prim,
The Methodist appear'd in him.

But, be his outward what it will,
His heart was an apostate's still.   30
He'd oft profess an hallow'd flame,
And ev'rywhere preach'd *Wesley's* name;
He was a preacher, and what not,
As long as money could be got;
He'd oft profess, with holy fire,   35
" The labourer's worthy of his hire."
   It happen'd once upon a time,
When all his works were in their prime,
A noble place appear'd in view;
Then – to the Methodists, adieu!   40
A Methodist no more he'll be,
The Protestants serve best for *he*.
Then to the curate straight he ran,
And thus address'd the rev'rend man :
" I was a Methodist, 'tis true;   45
With penitence I turn to you.
O that it were your bounteous will
That I the vacant place might fill!
With justice I'd myself acquit,
Do ev'ry thing that's right and fit."   50
The curate straightway gave consent –
To take the place he quickly went.
Accordingly he took the place,
And keeps it with dissembled grace.

To Horace Walpole

Walpole, I thought not I should ever see
So mean a heart as thine has prov'd to be.
Thou who, in luxury nurst, beholdst with scorn
The boy, who friendless, penniless, forlorn,

Asks thy high favour – thou mayst call me cheat.   5
Say, didst thou never practise such deceit?
Who wrote *Otranto*? but I will not chide :
Scorn I'll repay with scorn, and pride with pride.
Still, *Walpole,* still thy prosy chapters write,
And twaddling letters to some fair indite;   10
Laud all above thee, fawn and cringe to those
Who, for thy fame, were better friends than foes;
Still spurn the'incautious fool who dares – . . .

Had I the gifts of wealth and luxury shar'd,
Not poor and mean, *Walpole*! thou hadst not dar'd   15
Thus to insult.   But I shall live and stand
By *Rowley's* side, when thou art dead and damn'd.

Intended to have sent the above to Mr. Walpole but my Sister
perswaded me out of it.   T.C.

from '*Journal 6th*'

Say, *Baker,* if experience hoar
Has yet unbolted wisdom's door,
What is this phantom of the mind,
This love, when sifted and refin'd?
When the poor lover, fancy-frighted,   5
Is with his shadowy joys delighted,
A frown shall throw him in despair;
A smile shall brighten up his air.
Jealous without a seeming cause,
From flatt'ring smiles he misery draws;   10
Again, without his reason's aid,
His bosom's still, the devil's laid.
If this is love, my callous heart

27

Has never felt the rankling dart.
Oft have I seen the wounded swain 15
Upon the rack of pleasing pain,
Full of his flame, upon his tongue
The quivering declaration hung,
When lost to courage, sense, and reason,
He talked of weather and the season. 20
Such tremors never cower'd me,
I'm flatt'ring, impudent, and free,
Unmov'd by frowns and lowering eyes,
'Tis smiles I only ask and prize;
And when the smile is freely given, 25
You're in the highway-road to Heaven.
These coward lovers seldom find
That whining makes the ladies kind.
They laugh at silly silent swains
Who're fit for nothing but their chains. 30
'Tis an effrontery and tongue
On very oily hinges hung
Must win the blooming, melting fair,
And shew the joys of Heaven here.
    A rake, I take it, is a creature 35
Who winds through all the folds of nature;
Who sees the passions, and can tell
How the soft beating heart shall swell;
Who, when he ravishes the joy,
Defies the torments of the boy. 40
Who with the soul the body gains,
And shares love's pleasures, not his pains.
Who holds his charmer's reputation
Above a tavern veneration;
And when a love-repast he makes, 45
Not even prying fame partakes.
Who looks above a prostitute, he

28

Thinks love the only price of beauty,
And she that can be basely sold
Is much beneath or love or gold. 50
Who thinks the almost dearest part
In all the body is the heart :
Without it, rapture cannot rise,
Nor pleasures wanton in the eyes;
The sacred joy of love is dead, 55
Witness the sleeping marriage bed.
This is the picture of a rake,
Shew it the ladies – won't it take?
A buck's a beast of th'other side,
And real but in hoofs and hide : 60
To nature and the passions dead,
A brothel is his house and bed;
To fan the flame of warm desire,
And after wanton in the fire,
He thinks a labour; and his parts 65
Were not design'd to conquer hearts.
Serene with bottle, pox and whore
He's happy and requires no more.
The girls of virtue when he views,
Dead to all converse but the stews, 70
Silent as death, he's nought to say,
But sheepish steals himself away.
This is a buck to life display'd,
A character to charm each maid.
Now, prithee, friend, a choice to make, 75
Wouldst choose the buck before the rake?
The buck, as brutal as the name,
Invenoms every charmer's fame,
And though he never touch'd her hand,

Protests he had her at command.   80
The rake, in gratitude for pleasure,
Keeps reputation dear as treasure.

from *Elegy to the Memory of*
Mr. Thomas Phillips, of Fairford

No more I hail the morning's golden gleam,
No more the wonders of the view I sing;
Friendship requires a melancholy theme,
At her command the awful lyre I string!

Now as I wander through this leafless grove,   5
Where tempests howl, and blasts eternal rise,
How shall I teach the chorded shell to move,
Or stay the gushing torrent from my eyes?

Phillips! great master of the boundless lyre,
Thee would my soul-rack'd muse attempt to paint;   10
Give me a double portion of thy fire,
Or all the powers of language are too faint.

Say, soul unsullied by the filth of vice,
Say, meek-eyed spirit, where's thy tuneful shell
Which when the silver stream was lock'd with ice,   15
Was wont to cheer the tempest-ravag'd dell?

Oft as the filmy veil of ev'ning drew
The thick'ning shade upon the vivid green,
Thou, lost in transport at the dying view,
Bid'st the ascending Muse display the scene.   20

When golden Autumn, wreath'd in rip'ned corn,
From purple clusters prest the foamy wine,
Thy genius did his sallow brows adorn,
And made the beauties of the season thine.

With rustling sound the yellow foliage flies,   25
And wantons with the wind in rapid whirls;
The gurgling riv'let to the valley hies,
Whilst on its bank the spangled serpent curls.

The joyous charms of Spring delighted saw
Their beauties doubly glaring in thy lay;   30
Nothing was Spring which *Phillips* did not draw,
And every image of his Muse was May.

So rose the regal hyacinthal star,
So shone the verdure of the daisied bed,
So seem'd the forest glimm'ring from afar;   35
You saw the real prospect as you read.

Majestic Summer's blooming flow'ry pride
Next claim'd the honour of his nervous song;
He taught the stream in hollow trills to glide,
And led the glories of the year along.   40

Pale, rugged Winter bending o'er his tread,
His grizzled hair bedropt with icy dew;
His eyes, a dusky light congeal'd and dead,
His robe, a tinge of bright ethereal blue.

His train a motley'd, sanguine, sable cloud,   45
He limps along the russet, dreary moor,
Whilst rising whirlwinds, blasting, keen, and loud,
Roll the white surges to the sounding shore.

The rough October has his pleasures too;
But I'm insensible to every joy :
Farewell the laurel !   Now I grasp the yew,   55
And all my little pow'rs in grief employ.

       *   *   *   *   *

But see ! the sick'ning lamp of day retires,
And the meek ev'ning shades the dusty grey;
The west faint glimmers with the saffron fires,   95
And like thy life, O *Phillips* ! dies away.

Here, stretch'd upon this heav'n-ascending hill,
I'll wait the horrors of the coming night,
I'll imitate the gently-plaintive rill,
And by the glare of lambent vapours write.   100

Wet with the dew the yellow hawthorns bow;
The rustic whistles through the echoing cave;
Far o'er the lea the breathing cattle low,
And the full Avon lifts the darken'd wave.

       *   *   *   *   *

See ! See ! the pitchy vapour hides the lawn,
Nought but a doleful bell of death is heard,
Save where into a blasted oak withdrawn
The scream proclaims the curst nocturnal bird.   120

Now rest, my Muse, but only rest to weep
A friend made dear by ev'ry sacred tie;
Unknown to me be comfort, peace or sleep :
Phillips is dead – 'tis pleasure then to die.

Few are the pleasures *Chatterton* e'er knew,   125
Short were the moments of his transient peace;
But melancholy robb'd him of those few,
And this hath bid all future comforts cease.

And can the Muse be silent, *Phillips* gone?
And am I still alive?   My soul, arise!   130
The robe of immortality put on,
And meet thy *Phillips* in his native skies.

The Defence

No more, dear *Smith,* the hackney'd tale renew;
I own their censure, I approve it too.
For how can idiots, destitute of thought,
Conceive or estimate, but as they're taught?
Say, can the satirizing pen of *Shears*   5
Exalt his name, or mutilate his ears?
None but a *Lawrence* can adorn his lays,
Who in a quart of claret drinks his praise.
Taylor repeats what *Catcott* told before,
But lying *Taylor* is believ'd no more.   10
If in myself I think my notion just,
The Church and all her arguments are dust.
Religion's but Opinion's bastard son,
A perfect myst'ry, more than three in one.
'Tis fancy all, distempers of the mind;   15
As Education taught us, we're inclin'd.
Happy the man, whose reason bids him see
Mankind are by the state of nature free;
Who, thinking for himself, despises those

33

That would upon his better sense impose;   20
Is to himself the minister of God,
Nor treads the path where *Athanasius* trod.
Happy (if mortals can be) is the man,
Who not by priest, but Reason, rules his span :
Reason, to its possessor a sure guide;   25
Reason, a thorn in Revelation's side.
If Reason fails, incapable to tread
Through gloomy Revelation's thick'ning bed,
On what authority the Church we own?
How shall we worship deities unknown?   30
Can the Eternal Justice pleas'd receive
The pray'rs of those who, ignorant, believe?
Search the thick multitudes of ev'ry sect,
The Church supreme, with *Whitfield's* new elect;
No individual can their God define –   35
No, not great *Penny,* in his nervous line.
But why must *Chatterton* selected sit,
The butt of ev'ry critic's little wit?
Am I alone for ever in a crime,
Nonsense in prose, or blasphemy in rhyme?   40
All monosyllables a line appears :
Is it not very often so in *Shears?*
See gen'rous *Eccas* length'ning out my praise,
Enraptur'd with the music of my lays;
In all the arts of panegyric grac'd,   45
The cream of modern literary taste.
 " Why, to be sure, the metaphoric line
Has something sentimental, tender, fine;
But then, how hobbling are the other two –
There are some beauties, but they're very few.   50
Besides, the author (' faith, 'tis something odd !)
Commends a reverential awe of God.

Read but another fancy of his brain,
He's atheistical in ev'ry strain."
    Fallacious is the charge – 'tis all a lie.   55
As to my reason, I can testify,
I own a God, immortal, boundless, wise,
Who bid our glories of creation rise;
Who form'd his varied likeness in mankind,
Centring his many wonders in the mind;   60
Who saw Religion a fantastic night,
But gave us Reason, to obtain the light.
Indulgent *Whitfield* scruples not to say,
He only can direct to Heav'n's high-way;
While bishops with as much vehemence tell,   65
All sects heterodox are food for Hell.
    Why then, dear *Smith*, since doctors disagree,
Their notions are not oracles to me :
What I think right I ever will pursue,
And leave you liberty to do so too.   70

A Bacchanalian

What is war and all its joys?
Useless mischief, empty noise.
What are arms and trophies won?
Spangles glitt'ring in the sun.
Rosy Bacchus, give me wine,   5
Happiness is only thine!

What is love without the bowl?
'Tis a languor of the soul :
Crown'd with ivy, Venus charms,
Ivy courts me to her arms.   10

Bacchus, give me love and wine,
Happiness is only thine !

To Miss Hoyland

Go, gentle Muse, and to my fair one say,
My ardent passion mocks the feeble lay,
That love's pure flame my panting breast inspires,
And friendship warms me with her chaster fires.
Yes, more my fond esteem, my matchless love,   5
Than the soft turtle's, cooing in the grove;
More than the lark delights to mount the sky,
Then, sinking on the greensward, soft to lie;
More than the bird of eve, at close of day,
To pour in solemn solitude her lay;   10
More than grave *Camplin,* with his deep-ton'd note,
To mouth the sacred service got by rote;
More than sage *Catcott* does his storm of rain,
Sprung from th' abyss of his eccentric brain,
Or than his wild-antique and sputtering brother   15
Loves in his ale-house chair to drink and pother;
More than soft *Lewis,* that sweet pretty thing,
Loves in the pulpit to display his ring;
More than frail mortals love a brother sinner,
And more than Bristol aldermen their dinner,   20
When full four pounds of the well-fatten'd haunch
In twenty mouthfuls fill the greedy paunch.
   If these true strains can thy dear bosom move,
Let thy soft blushes speak a mutual love :
But if thy purpose settles in disdain,   25
Speak my dread fate, and bless thy favourite swain.

36

from *February: An Elegy*

Begin, my Muse, the imitative lay,
Aonian doxies sound the thrumming string;
Attempt no number of the plaintive *Gray*,
Let me like midnight cats, or *Collins* sing.

If in the trammels of the doleful line   5
The bounding hail, or drilling rain descend;
Come, brooding Melancholy, pow'r divine,
And ev'ry unform'd mass of words amend.

Now the rough Goat withdraws his curling horns,
And the cold Wat'rer twirls his circling mop;   10
Swift, sudden anguish darts through alt'ring corns,
And the spruce mercer trembles in his shop.

Now infant authors, madd'ning for renown,
Extend the plume and hum about the stage,
Procure a benefit, amuse the town,   15
And proudly glitter in a title-page.

Now, wrapt in ninefold fur, his squeamish grace
Defies the fury of the howling storm;
And, whilst the tempest whistles round his face,
Exults to find his mantled carcase warm.   20

Now rumbling coaches furious drive along,
Full of the majesty of city dames,
Whose jewels, sparkling in the gaudy throng,
Raise strange emotions and invidious flames.

*   *   *   *   *

Now – but what further can the Muses sing? 45
Now dropping particles of water fall;
Now vapours, riding on the north wind's wing,
With transitory darkness shadow all.

Alas! How joyless the descriptive theme,
When sorrow on the writer's quiet preys; 50
And, like a mouse in Cheshire cheese supreme,
Devours the substance of the lessening bays!

Come, February, lend thy darkest sky,
There teach the winter'd Muse with clouds to soar;
Come, February, lift the number high; 55
Let the sharp strain like wind through alleys roar.

Ye channels, wand'ring through the spacious street,
In hollow murmurs roll the dirt along,
With inundations wet the sabl'd feet,
Whilst gouts, responsive, join th'elegiac song. 60

Ye damsels fair, whose silver voices shrill
Sound through meandering folds of echo's horn,
Let the sweet cry of liberty be still,
No more let smoking cakes awake the morn.

O, Winter! put away thy snowy pride; 65
O, Spring! neglect the cowslip and the bell;
O, Summer! throw thy pears and plums aside;
O, Autumn! bid the grape with poison swell.

The pension'd muse of *Johnson* is no more!
Drown'd in a butt of wine his genius lies: 70
Earth! Ocean! Heav'n! the wondrous loss deplore,
The dregs of nature with her glory dies.

What iron Stoic can suppress the tear?
What sour reviewer reads with vacant eye?
What bard but decks his literary bier? 75
Alas! I cannot sing – I howl – I cry! . . .

The Art of Puffing

By a Bookseller's Journeyman

Vers'd by experience in the subtle art,
The myst'ries of a title I impart :
Teach the young author how to please the town,
And make the heavy drug of rhyme go down.
Since *Curl,* immortal, never-dying name! 5
A double Pica in the book of Fame,
By various arts did various dunces prop,
And tickled ev'ry fancy to his shop,
Who can, like *Pottinger,* ensure a book?
Who judges with the solid taste of *Cooke*? 10
Villains, exalted in the midway sky,
Shall live again to drain your purses dry :
Nor yet unrivall'd they; see *Baldwin* comes,
Rich in inventions, patents, cuts, and hums :
The honourable *Boswell* writes, 'tis true, – 15
What else can *Paoli's* supporters do?
The trading wits endeavour to attain,
Like booksellers, the world's first idol – gain.
For this they puff the heavy *Goldsmith's* line,
And hail his sentiment, though trite, divine; 20
For this the patriotic bard complains,
And *Bingley* binds poor Liberty in chains :
For this was ev'ry reader's faith deceiv'd,

And *Edmunds* swore what nobody believ'd :
For this the wits in close disguises fight;   25
For this the varying politicians write;
For this each month new magazines are sold,
With dullness fill'd and transcripts of the old.
The *Town and Country* struck a lucky hit,
Was novel, sentimental, full of wit :   30
Aping her walk the same success to find,
The *Court and City* hobbles far behind.
Sons of Apollo, learn : merit's no more
Than a good frontispiece to grace the door;
The author who invents a title well   35
Will always find his cover'd dullness sell :
Flexney and ev'ry bookseller will buy –
Bound in neat calf, the work will never die.

On the Immortality of the Soul

Say, O my soul, if not allow'd to be
Immortal, whence the mystery we see
Day after day, and hour after hour,
But to proclaim its never-ceasing power?
If not immortal, then our thoughts of thee   5
Are visions but of non-futurity.
Why do we live to feel of pain on pain,
If, in the midst of hope, we hope in vain?
Perish the thought in night's eternal shade :
To live, then die, man was not only made.   10
There's yet an awful something else remains
Either to lessen or increase our pains.
Whate'er it be, whate'er man's future fate,
Nature proclaims there is another state

Of woe, or bliss.   But who is he can tell?   15
None but the good, and they that have done well.
Oh! may that happiness be ours, my friend,
The little we have now will shortly end;
When joy and bliss more lasting will appear,
Or all our hopes translated into fear.   20
Oh! may our portion in that world above,
Eternal fountain of eternal love,
Be crown'd with peace that bids the sinner live;
With praise to Him who only can forgive –
Blot out the stains and errors of our youth;   25
Whose smile is mercy, and whose word is truth.

Rowley Poems

from Ælla

*A Tragycal Enterlude, or
Discoorseynge Tragedie,
wrotenn bie Thomas Rowleie;
Plaiedd before Mastre Canynge,
atte hys howse nempte the Rodde Lodge;
also before the Duke of Norfolck, Johan Howard.*
Personnes Representedd :
Ælla, bie Thomas Rowleie, Preeste, the Aucthoure.
Celmonde, Johan Iscamm, Preeste.
Hurra, Syrr Thybotte Gorges, Knyghte.
Birtha, Mastre Edwarde Canynge.
Odherr Partes bie Knyghtes, Mynstrelles.

Entroductionne

Somme cherisaunei 'tys to gentle mynde,	105
Whan heie have chevyced theyre londe from bayne,	
Whan theie ar dedd, theie leave yer name behynde,	
And theyre good deedes doe on the earthe remayne;	
Downe yn the grave wee ynhyme everych steyne,	
Whylest al her gentlenesse ys made to sheene,	110
Lyche fetyve baubels geasonne to be seene.	

Ælla, the wardenne of thys castell stede,	
Whylest Saxons dyd the Englysche sceptre swaie,	
Who made whole troopes of Dacyan men to blede,	
Then seel'd hys eyne, and seel'd hys eyne for aie,	115
Wee rowze hym uppe before the judgment daie,	

105 *cherisauni* comfort 106 *chevyced* preserved 109 *ynhyme* bury
111 *fetyve* beauteous; *baubels* jewels; *geasonne* rare 114 *Dacyan* Danish

42

To saie what he, as clergyond, can kenne,
And howe hee sojourned in the vale of men.

ÆLLA

The scene, Bristol.   Enter Celmonde.

CELMONDE :
Before yonne roddie sonne has droove hys wayne
Throwe halfe hys joornie, dyghte yn gites of goulde,   120
Mee, happeless mee, hee wylle a wretche behoulde,
Mieselfe, and al that's myne, bounde ynn myschaunces chayne.

Ah ! Birtha, whie dydde Nature frame thee fayre?
Whie art thou all thatt poyntelle canne bewreene?
Whie art thou nott as coarse as odhers are? –   125
Botte thenn thie soughle woulde throwe thy vysage sheene,
Yatt shemres onn thie comelie semlykeene,
Lyche nottebrowne cloudes, whann bie the sonne made redde,
Orr scarlette, wythe waylde lynnen clothe ywreene,
Syke would thie spryte uponn thie vysage spredde.   130
Thys daie brave Ælla dothe thyne honde and harte
Clayme as hys owne to be, whyche nee fromm hys moste parte.

And cann I lyve to see herr wythe anere?
Ytt cannotte, muste nott, naie, ytt shalle not bee.
Thys nyghte I'll putte stronge poysonn ynn the beere,   135
And hymm, herr, and myselfe, attenes wyll slea.
Assyst mee, Helle ! lett Devylles rounde mee tende,
To slea mieself, mie love, and eke mie doughtie friende.

117 *clergyond* taught   120 *dyghte* decked; *gites* robes   124 *poyntelle* pen;
bewreene describe   127 *shemres* shimmers; *seemlykeene* countenance   129
waylde choice; *ywreene* covered   130 *syke* so   133 *anere* another   136
attenes at once   138 *doughtie* mighty

Enter Ælla and Birtha.

ÆLLA :

Notte, whanne the hallie prieste dyd make me knyghte,
Blessynge the weaponne, tellynge future dede,   140
Howe bie mie honde the prevyd Dane should blede,
Howe I schulde often bee, and often wynne, ynn fyghte;

Notte, whann I fyrste behelde thie beauteous hue,
Whyche strooke mie mynde, and rouzed mie softer soule;
Nott, whann from the barbed horse yn fyghte dyd viewe   145
The flying Dacians oere the wyde playne roule,
Whan all the troopes of Denmarque made grete dole,
Dydd I fele joie wyth syke reddoure as nowe,
Whan hallie preest, the lechemanne of the soule,
Dydd knytte us both ynn a caytysnede vowe :   150
Now hallie Ælla's selynesse ys grate;
Shap haveth nowe ymade hys woes for to emmate.

BIRTHA :

Mie lorde, and husbande, syke a joie ys myne;
Botte mayden modestie moste ne soe saie,
Albeytte thou mayest rede ytt ynn myne eyne,   155
Or ynn myne harte, where thou shalte be for aie;
Inne sothe, I have botte meeded oute thie faie;
For twelve tymes twelve the mone hathe bin yblente,
As manie tymes hathe vyed the Godde of daie,
And on the grasse her lemes of sylverr sente,   160
Sythe thou dydst cheese mee for thie swote to bee,
Enactynge ynn the same moste faiefullie to mee.

139 *hallie* holy 141 *prevyd* warlike 145 *barbed* caparizoned 148 *reddoure*
violence 149 *lechemanne* physician 150 *caytysnede* binding 151 *selynesse*
happiness 152 *Shap* fate; *emmate* abate 155 *Albeytte* albeit; *eyne* eyes
157 *faie* faith 158 *yblente* blinded 160 *lemes* beams 161 *cheese* choose;
swote sweetheart

Ofte have I seene thee atte the none-daie feaste,
Whanne deysde bie thieselfe, for want of pheeres,
Awhylst thie merryemen dydde laughe and jeaste,   165
Onn mee thou semest all eyne, to mee all eares.
Thou wardest mee as gyff ynn hondred feeres,
Alest a daygnous looke to thee be sente,
And offrendes made mee, moe thann yie compheeres,
Offe scarpes of scarlette, and fyne parament;   170
All thie yntente to please was lyssed to mee,
I saie ytt, I moste streve thatt you ameded bee.

ÆLLA :
Mie lyttel kyndnesses whyche I dydd doe,
Thie gentleness doth corven them so grete,
Lyche bawsyn olyphauntes mie gnattes doe shewe;   175
Thou doest mie thoughtes of paying love amate;
Botte hann mie actyonns straughte the rolle of fate,
Pyghte thee fromm Hell, or broughte Heaven down to thee,
Layde the whol worlde a falldstole atte thie feete,
On smyle would be suffycyll mede for mee.   180
I amm Loves borro'r, and canne never paie,
Botte be hys borrower stylle, and thyne, mie swete, for aie.

BIRTHA :
Love, doe notte rate your achevmentes soe small;
As I to you, syke love untoe mee beare;
For nothynge paste wille Birtha ever call,   185
Ne on a foode from Heaven thynke to cheere.
As farr as thys frayle brutylle flesch wyll spere,
Syke, and ne fardher I expecte of you;

164 *deysde* on the dais; *pheeres* peers   167 *gyff* if   168 *daygnous* disdainful
169 *offrendes* offerings   170 *scarpes* scarves; *parament* robes   171 *lyssed*
devoted   172 *ameded* rewarded   174 *corven* carve, portray   175 *bawsyn*
great   176 *amate* defeat   177 *straughte* stretched out   178 *Pyghte* pulled
179 *falldstole* footstool

45

Be notte toe slacke yn love, ne overdeare;
A smalle fyre, yan a loude flame, proves more true.   190

ÆLLA :
Thie gentle wordis doe thie volunde kenne
To bee moe clergionde thann ys ynn meyncte of menne.

Enter   Minstrels

CELMONDE :
Alle blessynges showre on gentle Ælla's hedde!
Oft maie the moon, yn sylverr sheenynge lyghte,
Inn varied chaunges varyed blessynges shedde,   195
Besprengeynge far abrode mischaunces nyghte;
And thou, fayre Birtha! thou, fayre Dame, so bryghte,
Long mayest thou wyth Ælla fynde much peace,
Wythe selynesse, as wyth a roabe, be dyghte,
Wyth everych chaungynge mone new joies encrease!   200
I, as a token of mie love to speak,
Have brought you jubbes of ale, at nyghte youre brayne to breake.

ÆLLA :
Whan sopperes paste we'lle drenche youre ale soe stronge,
Tyde lyfe, tyde death.

CELMONDE :
             Ye Mynstrelles, chaunt your songe.

Mynstrelles Songe, bie a Manne and Womanne

MANNE :   Tourne thee to thie Shepsterr swayne;   205
           Bryghte sonne has ne droncke the dewe

190 *yan* than   191 *volunde* understanding   192 *clergionde* wise; *meyncte*
many   194 *sheenynge* shining   196 *Besprengeynge* scattering   199 *selynesse*
happiness; *dyghte* decked   202 *jubbes* bottles   205 *Shepsterr* shepherd

                      From the floures of yellowe hue;
                      Tourne thee, Alyce, backe again.
WOMANNE :   No, bestoikerre, I wylle goe,
                      Softlie tryppynge o'ere the mees,   210
                      Lyche the sylver-footed doe,
                      Seekeynge shelterr yn grene trees.
MANNE :   See the moss growne daisey'd banke,
                      Pereynge ynne the streme belowe;
                      Here we'lle sytte, yn dewie danke;   215
                      Tourne thee, Alyce, do notte goe.
WOMANNE :   I've hearde erste mie grandame saie,
                      Yonge damoyselles schulde ne bee,
                      Inne the swotie monthe of Maie,
                      Wythe yonge menne bie the grene wode tree.   220
MANNE :   Sytte thee, Alyce, sytte, and harke,
                      Howe the ouzle chauntes hys noate,
                      The chelandree, greie-morn larke,
                      Chauntynge from theyre lyttel throate;
WOMANNE :   I heare them from eche grene wode tree,   225
                      Chauntynge owte so blatauntlie,
                      Tellynge lecturnyes to mee,
                      Myscheefe ys whanne you are nygh.
MANNE :   See alonge the mees so grene
                      Pied daisies, kynge-coppes swote;   230
                      Alle we see, bie non bee seene,
                      Nete botte shepe settes here a fote.
WOMANNE :   Shepster swayne, you tare mie gratche.
                      Oute uponne ye! lette me goe.
                      Leave me swythe, or I'lle alatche.   235
                      Robynne, thys youre dame shall knowe.

209 *bestoikerre* deceiver   210 *mees* meadows   219 *swotie* sweet   222 *ouzle*
blackbird   223 *chelandree* goldfinch   226 *blatauntlie* loudly   227 *lecturnyes*
lectures   233 *tare* tear; *gratch* clothing   235 *swythe* at once; *alatche* call
out

47

MANNE :   See! the crokynge brionie
Rounde the popler twyste hys spraie;
Rounde the oake the greene ivie
Florryshcethe and lyveth aie.   240

Lette us seate us bie thys tree,
Laughe, and synge to lovynge ayres;
Comme, and doe notte coyen bee;
Nature made all thynges bie payres.

Drooried cattes wylle after kynde;   245
Gentle doves wylle kyss and coe :
WOMANNE : Botte manne, hee moste be ywrynde,
Tylle syr preeste make on of two.

Tempte me ne to the foule thynge;
I wylle no mannes lemanne be;   250
Tyll syr preeste hys songe doethe synge,
Thou shalt neere fynde aught of mee.
MANNE :   Bie our ladie her yborne,
To-morrowe, soone as ytte ys daie,
I'lle make thee wyfe, ne bee forsworne,   255
So tyde me lyfe or dethe for aie.
WOMANNE : Whatt dothe lette, botte thatte nowe
Wee attenes, thos honde yn honde,
Unto divinstre goe,
And bee lyncked yn wedlocke bonde?   260
MANNE :   I agree, and thus I plyghte
Honde, and harte, and all that's myne;
Goode syr Rogerr, do us ryghte,
Make us one, at Cothbertes shryne.

237 *crokynge* curling 243 *coyen* coy 245 *Drooried* chaste 247 *ywrynde*
covered up (i.e. celibate) 250 *lemanne* lover 257 *lette* hinder 258 *attenes*
at once 259 *divinstre* clergyman

Than to compare, as ye have done,
To match the candle with the sun.   30

17
When Windsor walls sustained my wearied arm,
My hand my chin, to ease my restless head,
Each pleasant spot revested green with warm,
The blossomed boughs with lusty Ver yspread,
The flowered meads, the wedded birds so late,   5
Mine eyes discovered. Then did to mind resort
The jolly woes, the hateless short debate,
The rakehell life that 'longs to love's disport.
Wherewith, alas, mine heavy charge of care
Heaped in my breast breaks forth against my will,   10
And smoky sighs that overcast the air.
My vapoured eyes such dreary tears distil
The tender spring to quicken where they fall,
And I half bent to throw me down withal.

18
So cruel a prison how could betide, alas,
As proud Windsor, where I, in lust and joy,
With a king's son my childish years did pass,
In greater feast than Priam's sons of Troy.

Where each sweet place returns a taste full sour.   5
The large green courts, where we were wont to hove,
With eyes cast up unto the maidens' tower,
And easy sighs, such as folk draw in love.

The stately sales; the ladies bright of hue,
The dances short, long tales of great delight,   10
With words and looks that tigers could but rue,
Where each of us did plead the other's right.

The evenynge commes, and brynges the dewe alonge,
The roddie welkynne sheeneth to the eyne;   285
Arounde the alestake Mynstrells synge the songe;
Yonge ivie rounde the doore poste do entwyne;
I laie mee onn the grasse; yette, to mie wylle,
Albeytte alle ys fayre, there lackethe somethynge stylle.

SECOND MYNSTRELLE:

So Adam thoughtenne, whann, ynn Paradyse,   290
All Heavenn and Erthe dyd hommage to hys mynde;
Ynn Womman alleyne mannes pleasaunce lyes;
As Instrumentes of joie were made the kynde.
Go, take a wyfe unto thie armes, and see
Wynter, and brownie hylles, wyll have a charme for thee.   295

THYRDE MYNSTRELLE:

Whanne Autumpne blake and sonne-brente doe appere,
With hys goulde honde guylteynge the falleynge lefe,
Bryngeynge oppe Wynterr to folfylle the yere,
Beerynge uponne hys backe the riped shefe;
Whan al the hyls wythe woddie sede ys whyte;   300
Whanne levynne-fyres and lemes do mete from far the syghte;

Whann the fayre apple, rudde as even skie,
Do bende the tree unto the fructyle ground;
When joicie peres, and berries of blacke die,
Doe daunce yn ayre, and call the eyne arounde;   305
Thann, bee the even foule, or even fayre,
Meethynckes mie hartys joie ys steynced wyth some care.

SECOND MYNSTRELLE:

Angelles bee wrogte to bee of neidher kynde;
Angelles alleyne fromme chafe desyre bee free;

285 *welkynne* sky   289 *Albeytte* albeit   296 *blake* bare   301 *levynne-fyres
and lemes* flashes of lightning   303 *fructyle* fertile   304 *joicie* juicy   307
steynced stained   309 *chafe* hot

Dherre ys a somewhatte evere yn the mynde, 310
Yatte, wythout wommanne, cannot stylled bee;
Ne seyncte yn celles, botte, havynge blodde and tere,
Do fynde the spryte to joie on syghte of womanne fayre :

Wommen bee made, notte for hemselves, botte manne,
Bone of hys bone, and chyld of hys desire; 315
Fromme an ynutyle membere fyrste beganne,
Yrwoghte with moche of water, lyttele fyre;
Therefore theie seke the fyre of love, to hete
The milkyness of kynde, and make hemselfes complete.

Albeytte, wythout wommen, menne were pheeres 320
To salvage kynde, and wulde botte lyve to slea,
Botte wommenne efte the spryghte of peace so cheres,
Tochelod yn Angel joie heie Angeles bee;
Go, take thee swythyn to thie bedde a wyfe,
Bee bante or blessed hie, yn proovynge marryage lyfe. 325

ÆLLA :
I lyche eke thys; goe ynn untoe the feaste; 350
Wee wylle permytte you antecedente bee;
There swotelie synge eche carolle, and yaped jeaste;
And there ys monnie, that you merrie bee;
Comme, gentle love, wee wylle toe spouse-feaste goe,
And there ynn ale and wyne bee dreyncted everych woe. 355

310 *somewhatte* something   312 *tere* health   316 *ynutyle* useless   320
pheeres equals   321 *salvage* savage   323 *Tochelod* embraced   324 *swythyn*
quickly   325 *bante* cursed   352 *yaped* comic   355 *dreyncted* drowned

Enter a Messenger.

MESSENGERE :

Ælla, the Danes ar thondrynge onn our coaste;
Lyche scolles of locusts, caste oppe bie the sea,
Magnus and Hurra, wythe a doughtie hoaste,
Are ragyng, to be quansed bie none botte thee;
Haste, swyfte as Levynne to these royners flee :   360
Thie dogges alleyne can tame thys ragynge bulle.
Haste swythyn, fore anieghe the towne theie bee,
And Wedecesterres rolle of dome bee fulle.
Haste, haste O Ælla, to the bycker flie,
For yn a momentes space tenne thousand menne maie die.   365

ÆLLA :
Beshrew thee for thie newes ! I moste be gon.
Was ever lockless dome so hard as myne !
Thos from dysportysmente to warr to ron,
To chaunge the selke veste for the gaberdyne !

BIRTHA :
O ! lyche a nedere, lette me rounde thee twyne,   370
And hylte thie boddie from the schaftes of warre.
Thou shalte nott, must not, from thie Birtha ryne,
Botte kenn the dynne of slughornes from afarre.

ÆLLA :
O love, was thys thie joie, to shewe the treate,
Than groffyshe to forbydde thie hongred guestes to eate?   375

359 *quansed* stopped   360 *Levynne* lightning; *royners* destroyers   362
swythyn swiftly   364 *bycker* conflict   369 *gaberdyne* armour   370 *nedere*
serpent   371 *hylte* shield   372 *ryne* run   373 *kenn* know (i.e. hear);
slughornes clarions   375 *groffyshe* churlishly

52

O mie upswalynge harte, whatt wordes can saie
The peynes, thatte passethe ynn mie soule ybrente?
Thos to bee torne uponne mie spousalle daie,
O! 'tys a peyne beyond entendemente.
Yee mychtie Goddes, and is yor favoures sente   380
As thous faste dented to a load of peyne?
Moste we aie holde yn chace the shade content,
And for a bodykin a swarthe obteyne?
O! whie, yee seynctes, oppress yee thos mie sowle?
How shalle I speke mie woe, mie freme, mie dreerie dole?   385

Celmonde :
Sometyme the wyseste lacketh pore mans rede.
Reasonne and counynge wytte efte flees awaie.
Thann, loverde, lett me saie, wyth hommaged drede
(Bieneth your fote ylayn) mie counselle saie;
Gyff thos we lett the matter lethlen laie,   390
The foemenn, everych honde-poyncte, getteth fote.
Mie loverde, lett the speere-menne, dyghte for fraie,
And all the sabbataners goe aboute.
I speke, mie loverde, alleyne to upryse
Youre wytte from marvelle, and the warriour to alyse.   395

Ælla :
Ah! nowe thou pottest takells yn mie harte;
Mie soulghe dothe nowe begynne to see herselle;
I wylle upryse mie myghte, and doe mie parte,
To slea the foemenne yn mie furie felle.
Botte howe canne tynge mie rampynge fourie telle,   400
Whyche ryseth from mie love to Birtha fayre?

377 *ybrente* burnt 379 *entendemente* understanding 381 *dented* coupled
383 *bodykin* body; *swarthe* shade 385 *freme* perplexity 386 *rede* wisdom
388 *loverde* lord 390 *lethlen* quiet 391 *honde-poyncte* minute 393
sabbataners foot-soldiers 395 *alyse* set free 396 *takells* arrows 400 *tynge*
tongue; *rampynge* raging

53

Ne could the queede, and alle the myghte of Helle,
Founde out impleasaunce of syke blacke a geare.
Yet I wylle bee mieselfe, and rouze mie spryte
To act wythe rennome, and goe meet the bloddie fyghte.   405

Birtha :
No, thou schalte never leave thie Birtha's syde;
Ne schall the wynde uponne us blowe alleyne;
I, lyche a nedre, wylle untoe thee byde;
Tyde lyfe, tyde deathe, ytte shall behoulde us twayne.
I have mie parte of drierie dole and peyne;   410
Itte brasteth from mee atte the holtred eyne;
Ynne tydes of teares mie swarthynge spryte wylle drayne,
Gyff drerie dole ys thyne, tys twa tymes myne.
Goe notte, O Ælla; wythe thie Birtha staie;
For wyth thie semmlykeed mie spryte wyll goe awaie.   415

Ælla :
O ! tys for thee, for thee alleyne I fele;
Yett I muste bee mieselfe; with valoures gear
I'lle dyghte mie hearte, and notte mie lymbes yn stele,
And shake the bloddie swerde and steyned spere.

Exeunt Ælla, Birtha and Messenger.

Celmonde :
Hope, hallie suster, sweepeynge thro' the skie,
In crowne of goulde, and robe of lillie whyte,
Whych farre abrode ynne gentle ayre do flie,
Meetynge from distaunce the enjoyous syghte,
Albeytte efte thou takest thie hie flyghte   510

402 *queede* devil   405 *rennome* honour   408 *nedre* serpent   411 *holtred*
covered   412 *swarthynge* dying   415 *semmlykeed* countenance

54

Hecket ynne a myste, and wyth thyne eyne yblente,
Nowe commest thou to mee wythe starrie lyghte;
Ontoe thie veste the rodde sonne ys adente;
The Sommer tyde, the month of Maie appere,
Depycte wythe skylledd honde uponn thie wyde aumere.   515

I from a nete of hopelen am adawed,
Awhaped atte the fetyveness of daie;
Ælla, bie nete moe thann hys myndbruche awed,
Is gone, and I moste followe, toe the fraie.
Celmonde canne ne'er from anie byker staie.   520
Dothe warre begynne? theres Celmonde yn the place.
Botte whanne the warre ys donne, I'll haste awaie.
The reste from nethe tymes masque must shew yttes face.
I see onnombered joies around mee ryse;
Blake stondethe future doome, and joie dothe mee alyse.   525

O honnoure, honnoure, whatt ys bie thee hanne?
Hailie the robber and the bordelyer,
Who kens ne thee, or ys to thee bestanne,
And nothynge does thie myckle gastness fere.
Faygne would I from mie bosomme alle thee tare.   530
Thou there dysperpellest thie levynne- bronde;
Whyllest mie soulgh's forwyned, thou art the gare;
Sleene ys mie comforte bie thie ferie honde;
As somme talle hylle, whann wynds doe shake the ground,
Itte kerveth all abroade, bie brasteynge hyltren wounde.   535

---

511 *Hecket* wrapped; *yblente* blinded   513 *adente* attached   515 *aumere*
mantle   516 *nete* night; *hopelen* hopelessness; *adawed* awakened   517
Awhaped astonished; *fetyveness* beauty   518 *myndbruche* honour   520
byker battle   525 *Blake* bare; *alyse* set free   526 *hanne* gained   527 *Hailie*
happy; *bordelyer* bawd   528 *bestanne* indifferent   531 *dysperpellest*
scatterest; *levynne-bronde* lightning flash   532 *forwyned* dried-up; *gare*
cause   535 *kerveth* cuts; *brasteynge* bursting open; *hyltren* hidden

Honnoure, whatt bee ytte? tys a shadowes shade,
A thynge of wychencref, an idle dreme;
On of the fonnis whych the clerche have made
Menne wydhoute sprytes, and wommen for to fleme;
Knyghtes, who efte kenne the loude dynne of the beme,   540
Schulde be forgarde to syke enfeeblynge waies,
Make everych acte, alyche theyr soules, be breme,
And for theyre chyvalrie alleyne have prayse.

      O thou, whatteer thie name,
      Or Zabalus or Queed,   545
      Comme, steel mie sable spryte,
      For fremde and dolefulle dede.

The Danish Camp, near Watchet. Magnus, Hurra and High Priest.

MAGNUS :
Swythe lette the offrendes to the Goddes begynne,
To knowe of hem the issue of the fyghte.
Potte the blodde-steyned sword and pavyes ynne;   550
Spreade swythyn all arounde the hallie lyghte.

Hie Preeste syngeth :

Yee, who hie yn mokie ayre
Delethe seasonnes foule or fayre,
Yee, who, whanne yee weere agguylte,
The mone yn bloddie gytelles hylte,   555
Mooved the starres, and dyd unbynde
Everyche barriere to the wynde;
Whanne the oundynge waves dystreste,
Storven to be overest,

538 *fonnis* frauds; *clerche* clergy   539 *fleme* frighten   540 *beme* trumpet
541 *forgarde* indifferent   542 *breme* fierce   547 *fremde* strange   548
offrendes sacrifices   550 *pavyes* shield   554 *agguylte* offended   555 *gytelles*
mantels   558 *oundynge* billowing   559 *Storven* strove; *overest* uppermost

56

Sockeynge yn the spyre-gyrte towne,   560
Swolterynge wole natyons downe,
Sendynge dethe, on plagues astrodde,
Moovynge lyke the erthys Godde;
To mee send your heste dyvyne,
Lyghte eletten all myne eyne,   565
Thatt I maie now undevyse
All the actyonnes of th'emprize.

falleth downe and eft rysethe.

Thus sayethe the Goddes; goe, yssue to the playne;
Forr there shall meynte of mytte menn be slayne.

MAGNUS :
Whie, soe there evere was, whanne Magnus foughte.   570
Efte have I treynted noyance throughe the hoaste,
Athorowe swerdes, alyche the Queed dystraughte,
Have Magnus pressynge wroghte hys foemen loaste.
As whanne a tempeste vexethe soar the coaste,
The dyngeynge ounde the sandeie stronde doe tare,   575
So dyd I inne the warre the javlynne toste,
Full meynte a champyonnes breaste received mie spear.
Mie sheelde, lyche sommere morie gronfer droke,
Mie lethalle speere, alych a levyn-mylted oke.

HURRA :
Thie wordes are greate, full of hyghe sound, and eeke   580
Lyche thonderre, to the whych dothe comme no rayne.
Itte lacketh notte a doughtie honde to speke;
The cocke saiethe drefte, yett armed ys he alleyne.

561 *Swolterynge* swallowing 565 *eletten* enlighten 566 *undevyse* perceive
569 *meynte* many; *mytte* mighty 571 *treynted* scattered; *noyance* injury
572 *Queed* Devil 575 *ounde* wave 576 *toste* throw 578 *morie* marshy;
gronfer fen-fire; *droke* thrust forward 579 *levyn-mylted* struck by lightning
583 *drefte* least

Certis thie wordes maie, thou motest have sayne
Of mee, and meynte of woe, who eke canne fyghte,   585
Who haveth trodden downe the adventayle,
And tore the heaulmes from heades of myckle myghte.
Sythence syke myghte ys placed yn thie honde,
Lette blowes thie actyons speeke, and bie thie corrage stonde.

---

*Battle is joined, and the Danes are defeated. Ælla, however, is
wounded.*

The scene, near Watchet. Enter Celmonde, followed by a Squire.

CELMONDE :
Mie servant squyre !   Prepare a fleing horse,
Whose feete are wynges, whose pace ys lycke the wynde,
Whoe wylle outestreppe the morneynge lyghte yn course,
Leaveynge the gyttelles of the merke behynde.
Somme hyltren matters doe mie presence fynde.   925
Gyv oute to alle yatte I was sleene ynne fyghte.
Gyff ynne thys gare thou doest mie order mynde,
Whanne I returne, thou shalte be made a knyghte;
Flie, flie, be gon; an howerre ys a daie;
Quycke dyghte mie best of stedes, and brynge hymm heere –
                                                            awaie !   930
Exit Squire.

Ælla ys woundedd sore, and ynne the toune
He waytethe, tylle hys woundes be broghte to ethe.
And shalle I from hys browes plocke off the croune,
Makynge the victore yn hys vyctorie blethe?

586 *adventayle* armour 587 *heaulmes* helmets 924 *gytelles* mantels
925 *hyltren* hidden; *fynde* require 927 *Gyff* if; *gare* matter 932 *ethe*
ease   934 *blethe* bleed

O no! fulle sooner schulde mie hartes blodde smethe,   935
Fulle soonere woulde I tortured bee to deathe;
Botte– Birtha ys the pryze; ahe! ytte were ethe
To gayne so gayne a pryze wythe losse of breathe;
Botte thanne rennome aeterne – ytte ys botte ayre;
Bredde ynne the phantasie, and alleyn lyvynge there.   940
Exit

The scene, Bristol.   Enter Birtha and Egwina.
BIRTHA :
Gentle Egwina, do notte preche me joie;
I cannotte joie ynne anie thynge botte weere.
Oh! yatte aughte schulde oure selynesse destroie,
Floddynge the face wythe woe, and brynie teare!

EGWINA :
You muste, you muste endeavour for to cheere   955
Youre harte unto somme cherisaunied reste.
Youre loverde from the battelle wylle appere,
 Ynne honnoure, and a greater love, be dreste :
Botte I wylle call the mynstrelles roundelaie;
Perchaunce the swotie sounde maie chase your wiere awaie.   960

Enter   Mynstrelles.

MYNSTRELLES SONG :
O! synge untoe mie roundelaie,
•O! droppe the brynie teare wythe mee,

935 *smethe* smoke   937 *ethe* easy   938 *so gayne* so fair   939 *rennome*
renoun   952 *weere* grief   953 *selynesse* happiness   956 *cherisaunied*
comforting   957 *loverde* lord

59

Daunce ne moe atte hallie daie,
Lycke a reyneynge ryver bee;
    Mie love ys dedde,   965
    Gon to hys death-bedde,
    Al under the wyllowe tree.

Blacke hys cryne as the wynter nyghte,
Whyte hys rode as the sommer snowe,
Rodde hys face as the morning lyghte,   970
Cale he lyes ynne the grave belowe;
    Mie love ys dedde,
    Gon to hys death-bedde,
    Al under the wyllowe tree.

Swote hys tynge as the throstles note,   975
Quycke ynn daunce as thoughte canne bee,
Defte hys taboure, codgelle stote,
O ! hee lyes bie the wyllowe tree :
    Mie love ys dedde,
    Gonne to hys deathe-bedde,   980
    Alle underre the wyllowe tree.

Harke ! the ravenne flappes hys wynge,
In the briered delle belowe;
Harke ! the dethe-owle loude dothe synge,
To the nyghte-mares as heie goe;   985
    Mie love ys dedde,
    Gonne to hys deathe-bedde,
    Al under the wyllowe tree.

See ! the whyte moone sheenes onne hie;
Whyterre ys mie true loves shroude;   990

968 *cryne* hair   969 *rode* complexion   971 *Cale* cold   977 *stote* stout

Whyterre yanne the mornynge skie,
Whyterre yanne the evenynge cloude;
    Mie love ys dedde,
    Gon to hys deathe-bedde,
    Al under the wyllowe tree.   995

Here, uponne mie true loves grave,
Schalle the baren fleurs be layde,
Nee one hallie Styncte to save
Al the celness of a mayde.
    Mie love ys dedde,   1000
    Gonne to hys death-bedde,
    Alle under the wyllowe tree.

Wythe mie hondes I'lle dente the brieres
Rounde hie hallie corse to gre,
Ouphante fairie, lyghte youre fyres,   1005
Heere mie boddie stylle schalle bee.
    Mie love ys dedde,
    Gon to hys death-bedde,
    Al under the wyllowe tree.

Comme, wythe acorne-coppe and thorne,   1010
Drayne mie hartys blodde awaie;
Lyfe and all yttes goode I scorne,
Daunce bie nete, or feaste by daie.
    My love ys dedde,
    Gon to hys death-bedde,   1015
    Al under the wyllowe tree.

Waterre wytches, crownede wythe reytes,
Bere mee to yer leathalle tyde.

999 *celness* coldness   1003 *dente* twine   1004 *gre* grow   1005 *Ouphante* elphin   1017 *reytes* rushes

61

I die; I comme; mie true love waytes.
Thos the damselle spake, and dyed.   1020

BIRTHA :
Thys syngeyng haveth whatte coulde make ytte please;
Butte mie uncourtlie shappe benymmes mee of all ease.

Exeunt.

The scene, Bristol.   Celmonde alone.

CELMONDE :
The worlde ys darke wythe nyghte; the wyndes are stylle;
Fayntelie the mone her palyde lyght makes gleme;
The upryste sprytes the sylente letten fylle,   1045
Wythe ouphant faeryes joynyng ynne the dreme;
The forreste sheenethe wythe the sylver leme;
Now maie mie love be sated ynn yttes treate;
Uponne the lynche of somme swefte reynyng streme,
Att the swote banquette I wylle swotelie eate.   1050
Thys ys the howse; yee hyndes, swythyn appere.

Enter   Servytoure.

CELMONDE :
Go telle to Birtha strayte, a straungerr waytethe here.

Enter   Birtha.

BIRTHA :
Celmonde ! yee seynctes ! I hope thou haste goode newes.

1022 *shappe* fate; *benymmes* deprives   1045 *upryste* uprisen; *letten* church-
yard   1046 *ouphant* elphin   1047 *leme* gleam   1049 *lynche* bank   1051
hyndes servants; *swythyn* swiftly

CELMONDE :
The hope ys loste; for heavie newes prepare.

BIRTHA :
Is Ælla welle?

CELMONDE :
        Hee lyves; and stylle maie use   1055
The behylte blessynges of a future yeare.

BIRTHA :
Whatte heavie tydynge thenne have I to feare?
Of whatte mischaunce dydste thou so latelie saie?

CELMONDE :
For heavie tydynges swythyn nowe prepare.
Ælla sore wounded ys, yn bykerous fraie;   1060
In Wedecesters wallid toune he lyes.

BIRTHA :
O mie agroted breast!

CELMONDE :
        Wythoute your syghte, he dyes.

BIRTHA :
Wylle Birtha's presence ethe herr Ælla's payne?
I fflie; newe wynges doe from mie schoulders sprynge.

CELMONDE :
Mie stede wydhoute wylle deftlie beere us twayne.   1065

1056 *behylte* promised 1059 *swythyn* quickly 1060 *bykerous* violent
1062 *agroted* stifled 1063 *ethe* ease

BIRTHA :

Oh! I wyll flie as wynde, and no waie lynge;
Sweftlie caparisons for rydynge brynge;
I have a mynde wynged wythe the levyne ploome.
O Ælla, Ælla! dydste thou kenne the stynge,
The whyche doeth canker ynne mie hartys roome,   1070
Thou wouldste see playne thieself the gare to bee;
Aryse, uponne thie love, and flie to meeten mee.

CELMONDE :

The stede, on whyche I came, ys swefte as ayre;
Mie servytoures doe wayte mee nere the wode;
Swythynne wythe mee unto the place repayre;   1075
To Ælla I wylle gev you conducte goode.
Youre eyne, alyche a baulme wylle staunche hys bloode,
Holpe oppe hys woundes, and yev hys harte alle cheere;
Uponne your eyne he holdes hys lyvelyhode;
You doe hys spryte, and alle hys pleasaunce bere.   1080
Comme, lette's awaie, albeytte ytte ys moke,
Yette love wille bee a tore tourne to feere nyghtes smoke.

A Forest.   Enter Celmonde and Birtha.

BIRTHA :

Thys merkness doe affraie mie wommanns breaste.
Howe sable ys the spreddynge skie arrayde!
Hallie the bordeleire, who lyves to reste,   1125
Ne ys att nyghtys flemynge hue dysmayde;
The starres doe scantillie the sable brayde;

1066 *lynge* delay   1068 *levyn* lightning   1071 *gare* cause   1080 *bere* bear
1081 *moke* much   1082 *tore* torch   1125 *bordeleire* cottager   1126 *flemynge*
fearsome

Wyde ys the sylver lemes of comforte wove;
Speke, Celmonde, does ytte make thee notte afrayde?

CELMONDE :
Merker the nyghte, the fitter tyde for love.   1130

BIRTHA :
Saiest thou for love? ah ! love is far awaie.
Faygne would I see once moe the roddie lemes of daie.

CELMONDE :
Love maie bee nie, woulde Birtha calle ytte here.

BIRTHA :
How, Celmonde, dothe thou mene?

CELMONDE :
     Thys Celmonde menes.
No leme, no eyne, ne mortalle manne appere,   1135
Ne lyghte, an acte of love for to bewreene;
Nete in thys forreste, botte thys tore, dothe sheene,
The whych, potte oute, do leave the whole yn nyghte;
See ! howe the brauncynge trees doe here entwyne,
Makeynge thys bower so pleasynge to the syghte;   1140
Thys was for love fyrste made, and heere ytt stondes,
Thatte hereynne lovers maie enlyncke yn true loves bandes.

BIRTHA :
Celmonde, speake whatte thou menest, or alse mie thoughtes
Perchance maie robbe thie honestie so fayre.

CELMONDE :
Then here, and knowe, hereto I have you broughte,   1145
Mie longe hydde love unto you to make clere.

1128 *lemes* gleams   1130 *merker* darker   1136 *bewreene* reveal   1137 *Nete*
nought; *tore* torch

65

BIRTHA :

Oh heaven and earthe! whatte ys ytt I doe heare?
Am I betraste? where ys mie Ælla, saie!

CELMONDE :

O! do nete nowe to Ælla syke love bere,
Botte geven some onn Celmondes hedde.   1150

BIRTHA :

                              Awaie!
I wylle be gone, and groape mie passage oute,
Albeytte neders stynges mie legs do twyne aboute.

CELMONDE :

Nowe bie the seynctes I wylle notte lette thee goe,
Ontylle thou doeste mie brendynge love amate.
Those eyne have caused Celmonde myckle woe,   1155
Yenne lette yer smyle fyrst take hymm yn regrate.
O! didst thou see mie breastis troblous state,
There love doth harrie up mie joie, and ethe!
I wretched bee, beyond the hele of fate,
Gyff Birtha stylle wylle make mie harte-veynes blethe. 1160
Softe as the sommer flowreets, Birtha, looke,
Fulle ylle I canne thie frownes and harde dyspleasaunce brooke.

BIRTHA :

Thie love ys foule; I woulde bee deafe for aie,
Radher thanne heere syche deslavatie sedde.
Swythynne flie from mee, and ne further saie;   1165
Radher thanne heare thie love, I woulde bee dead.
Yee seynctes! and shal I wronge mie Ælla's bedde,

1148 *betraste* betrayed 1152 *neders* adders' 1154 *brendynge* burning;
amate quench 1156 *regrate* favour 1160 *blethe* bleed 1164 *deslavatie*
dishonour

And wouldst thou, Celmonde, tempte me to the thynge?
Lett mee be gone – alle curses onne thie hedde!
Was ytte for thys thou dydste a message brynge! 1170
Lette mee be gone, thou manne of sable harte!
Or welkyn and her starres will take a maydens parte.

CELMONDE:
Sythence you wylle notte lette mie suyte avele,
Mie love wylle have yttes joie, altho wythe guylte;
Youre lymbes shall bende, albeytte strynge as stele; 1175
The merkye seesonne wylle your bloshes hylte.

BIRTHA:
Holpe, holpe, yee seynctes! oh thatte mie blodde was spylte!

CELMONDE:
The seynctes att distaunce stonde ynn tyme of nede.
Strev notte to goe; thou canste notte, gyff thou wylte.
Untoe mie wysche bee kinde, and nete alse hede. 1180

BIRTHA:
No, foule bestoykerre, I wylle rende the ayre,
Tylle dethe do staie mie dynne, or somme kynde roder heare.
Holpe! holpe! oh Godde!

Enter Hurra and Danes, fleeing from the battlefield.

HURRA:
          Ah! thatt's a wommanne cries.
I kenn hem; saie, who are you, yatte bee theere?

1172 *welkyn* Heaven 1173 *avele* avail 1175 *strynge* strong 1180 *nete alse* nought else 1181 *bestoykerre* traitor 1182 *roder* rider

CELMONDE :
Yee hyndes, awaie! orre bie thys swerde yee dies.   1185

HURRA :
Thie wordes wylle ne mie hartis sete affere.

BIRTHA :
Save mee, oh! save mee from thys royner heere!

HURRA :
Stonde thou bie mee; nowe saie thie name and londe;
Or swythyne schall mie swerde thie boddie tare.

CELMONDE :
Bothe I wylle shewe thee bie mie brondeous honde.   1190

HURRA :
Besette hym rounde, yee Danes.

CELMONDE :
                              Comme onne, and see
Gyff mie strynge anlace maie bewryen whatte I bee.

All fight against Celmonde; he kills many, but falls to Hurra.

*Recognising that Ælla is an honourable and merciful enemy, the
Danes decide to escort his wife safely to Bristol.*

———————————————

1187 *royner* ravisher   1190 *brondeous* furious   1192 *strynge* strong; *anlace*
knife; *bewryen* reveal

Ælla, meanwhile, hears that Birtha has been seen leaving Bristol with a man. His faith in her constancy is shaken.

Bristol. Enter Ælla, then a Servant, and Coernyke.

SERVANT:
Loverde! I am aboute the trouthe to saie.　　　　　　　1295
Laste nyghte, fulle late I dydde retourne to reste.
As to mie chamber I dydde bende mie waie,
To Birtha onne hys name and place addreste;
Downe to hym camme shee; butte thereof the reste
I ken ne matter; so, mie hommage made –　　　　　　1300

ÆLLA:
O! speake ne moe; mie harte flames yn yttes keste;
I once was Ælla; nowe bee notte yttes shade.
Hanne alle the fuirie of mysfortunes wylle
Fallen onne mie benned headde I hanne been Ælla stylle.
Thys alleyn was unburled of alle mie spryte;　　　　1305
Mie honnoure, honnoure, frownd on the dolce wynde,
Thatte steeked on ytte; nowe wyth rage Im pyghte;
A brondeous unweere ys mie engyned mynde.
Mie hommeur yette somme drybblet joie maie fynde,
To the Danes woundes I wylle another yeve;　　　　1310
Whanne thos mie rennome and mie peace ys rynde,
Itte were a recrandize to thyncke toe lyve;
Mie huscarles, untoe everie asker telle,
Gyffe noblie Ælla lyved, as noblie Ælla felle.

Stabbeth hys breste.

1295 *Loverde* lord　1298 *onne* one　1301 *keste* chest　1302 *yttes* his　1304 *benned* cursed　1305 *unburled* unprotected　1306 *dolce* soft　1307 *steeked* followed; *pyghte* tortured　1308 *brondeous* furious; *unweere* tempest; *engyned* tormented　1311 *rennome* honour; *rynde* ruined　1312 *recrandize* dishonour　1313 *huscarles* servants

69

SERVANT:
Ælla ys sleene; the flower of Englond's marrde! 1315

ÆLLA:
Be stylle; stythe lette the chyrches rynge mie knelle.
Call hyther brave Coernyke; he, as warde
Of thys mie Brystowe castle, wyll doe welle.

Knelle ryngeth.

Enter Birtha and Hurra

ÆLLA:
Ah! Birtha here! 1325

BIRTHA:
Whatte dynne ys thys? Whatte menes yis leathalle knelle?
Where ys mie Ælla? speeke; where? howe ys hee?
Oh Ælla! art thou yanne alyve and well!

ÆLLA:
I lyve yndeed; botte doe notte lyve for thee.

BIRTHA:
Whatte menes mie Ælla?

ÆLLA:
                        Here mie meneynge see. 1330
Thie foulness urged mie honde to gyve thys wounde,
Ytte mee unsprytes.

1316 *stythe* quickly   1332 *unsprytes* un-spirits

70

BIRTHA :

Ytte hathe unspryted mee.

ÆLLA :

Ah heavens! mie Birtha fallethe to the grounde!
Botte yette I am a manne, and so wylle bee.

HURRA :

Ælla! I amme a Dane; botte yette a friende to thee.   1335
Thys damoyselle I founde wythynne a woode,
Strevynge fulle harde anenste a burled swayne;
I sente hym myrynge ynne mie compheeres blodde,
Celmonde hys name, chief of thie warrynge trayne.
Yis damoiselle soughte to be here agayne;   1340
The whyche, albeytte foemen, wee dydd wylle;
So here wee broughte her wythe you to remayne.

COERNYKE :

Yee nobylle Danes! wythe goulde I wyll you fylle.

ÆLLA :

Birtha, mie lyfe! mie love! oh! she ys fayre.   1344
Whatte faultes could Birtha have, whatte faultes could Ælla feare?

BIRTHA :

Amm I yenne thyne? I cannotte blame thie feere.
Botte doe reste mee uponne mie Ælla's breaste;
I wylle to thee bewryen the woefulle gare.
Celmonde dyd comme to mee at tyme of reste,
Wordeynge for mee to flie, att your request,   1350

1337 *anenste* against; *burled* armed   1338 *myrynge* wallowing; *compheeres*
companions   1348 *bewyren* reveal; *gare* cause   1350 *Wordeynge* demanding

71

To Watchette towne, where you deceasynge laie;
I wyth hym fledde; thro' a murke wode we preste,
Where hee foule love unto mie eares dyd saie;
The Danes –

ÆLLA :

      Oh ! I die content. –
dieth.

BIRTHA :

               Oh ! ys mie Ælla dedde?
O ! I will make hys grave mie vyrgyn spousal bedde.   1355

Birtha feyncteth.

COERNYKE :
Whatt? Ælla deadde ! and Birtha dyynge toe !
Soe falles the fayrest flourettes of the playne.
Who canne unplyte the wurchys heaven can doe?
Or who untweste the role of shappe yn twayne?
Ælla, thie rennome was thie onlie gayne;   1360
For yatte, thie pleasaunce, and thie joie was loste.
Thie countrymen shall rere thee, on the playne,
A pyle of carnes, as anie grave can boaste;
Further, a just amede to thee to bee,   1364
Inne heaven thou synge of Godde, on erthe we'lle synge of thee.

The Ende

1358 *unplyte* explain; *wurchys* works   1359 *shappe* fate   1363 *carnes* stones
1364 *amede* reward

An Excelente Balade of Charitie

As wroten bie the goode Prieste Thomas Rowley, 1464

In Virgyne the sweltrie sun gan sheene,
And hotte upon the mees did caste his raie;
The apple rodded from its palie greene
And the mole peare did bende the leafy spraie;
The peede chelandrie sunge the livelong daie;   5
'Twas nowe the pride, the manhood of the yeare,
And eke the grounde was dighte in its most defte aumere.

The sun was glemeing in the midde of daie,
Deadde still the aire, and eke the welken blue,
When from the sea arist in drear arraie   10
A hepe of cloudes of sable sullen hue,
The which full fast unto the woodlande drewe,
Hiltring attenes the sunnis fetive face,
And the blacke tempeste swolne and gatherd up apace.

Beneathe an holme, faste by a pathwaie side,   15
Which dide unto Seyncte Godwine's covent lede,
A hapless pilgrim moneynge did abide,
Pore in his viewe, ungentle in his weede,
Longe bretful of the miseries of neede;
Where from the hail-stone coulde the almer flie?   20
He had no housen theere, ne anie covent nie.

1 *sweltrie* sultry 2 *mees* meadows 3 *rodded* reddened 4 *mole* soft
5 *peede* pied; *chelandrie* goldfinch 7 *aumere* dress 13 *Hiltring* hiding;
attenes at once; *fetive* beautiful 15 *holme* oak 16 *covent* convent 18 *viewe*
appearance 19 *bretful* full up 20 *almer* beggar

Look in his glommed face, his sprighte there scanne;
Howe woe-be-gone, how withered, forwynd, deade!
Haste to thie church-glebe-house, asshrewed manne!
Haste to thie kiste, thie onlie dortoure bedde.   25
Cale, as the claie whiche will gre on thie hedde,
Is Charitie and Love aminge highe elves;
Knightis and Barons live for pleasure and themselves.

The gatherd storme is rype; the bigge drops falle;
The forswat meadowes smethe, and drenche the raine;   30
The comyng ghastness do the cattle pall,
And the full flockes are drivynge ore the plaine;
Dashde from the cloudes the waters flott againe;
The welkin opes; the yellow levynne flies;
And the hot fierie smothe in the wide lowings dies.   35

Liste! now the thunder's rattling clymmynge sound
Cheves slowlie on, and then embollen clangs,
Shakes the hie spyre, and losst, dispended, drown'd,
Still on the gallard eare of terroure hanges;
The windes are up; the lofty elmen swanges;   40
Again the levynne and the thunder poures,
And the full cloudes are braste attenes in stonen showers.

Spurreynge his palfrie oere the watrie plaine,
The Abbote of Seyncte Godwynes convente came;
His chapournette was drented with the reine,   45
And his pencte gyrdle met with mickle shame;
He ayneward tolde his bederoll at the same;

22 *glommed* dejected 23 *forwynd* withered 24 *church-glebe-house* grave;
asshrewed accursed 25 *kiste* coffin; *dortoure* sleeping-place 26 *Cale* cold;
gre grow 27 *elves* folk 30 *forswat* burnt; *smethe* steam; *drenche* drink
31 *ghastness* terror; *pall* appall 35 *smothe* vapour; *lowings* flames 36
clymmynge noisy 37 *Cheves* moves; *embollen* swollen 39 *gallard* terrified
40 *elmen* elm 41 *levynne* lightning 42 *stonen* stony 45 *chapournette*
cap; *drented* drenched 46 *pencte* dyed 47 *aynewarde tolde his bederoll*
told his beads backwards, i.e. cursed

74

The storme encreasen, and he drew aside,
With the mist almes craver neere to the holme to bide.

His cope was all of lyncolne clothe so fyne,   50
With a gold button fasten'd neere his chynne;
His autremete was edged with golden twynne,
And his shoone pyke a loverds mighte have binne;
Full well it shewn he thoughten coste no sinne;
The trammels of the palfrye pleasd his sighte,   55
For the horse-millanare his head with roses dighte.

An almes, sir prieste; the droppynge pilgrim saide,
O! let me waite within your covente dore,
Till the sunne sheneth hie above our heade,
And the loude tempeste of the aire is oer;   60
Helpless and ould am I alas! and poor;
No house, ne friend, ne moneie in my pouche;
All yatte I call my owne is this my silver crouche.

Varlet, replyd the Abbatte, cease your dinne;
This is no season almes and prayers to give;   65
Mie porter never lets a faitour in;
None touch mie rynge who not in honour live.
And now the sonne with the blacke cloudes did stryve,
And shettynge on the grounde his glairie raie,
The Abbatte spurrde his steede, and eftsoones roadde awaie.   70

Once moe the skie was blacke, the thunder rolde;
Faste reyneynge oer the plaine a prieste was seen;
Ne dighte full proude, ne buttoned up in golde;

49 *mist* poor; *holme* oak 52 *autremete* cloak 53 *shoon pyke* shoe-points;
loverds lord's 56 *horse-millanare* maker of horse-trappings 63 *crouche*
cross 66 *faitour* beggar 69 *shettynge* shedding; *raie* gaze

75

His cope and jape were graie, and eke were cleene;
A Limitoure he was of order seene;   75
And from the pathwaie side then turned hee,
Where the pore almer laie binethe the holmen tree.

An almes, sir priest! the dropping pilgrim sayde,
For sweete Seyncte Marie and your order sake.
The Limitoure then loosen'd his pouche threade,   80
And did thereoute a groate of silver take;
The mister pilgrim dyd for halline shake.
Here take this silver, it maie eathe thie care;
We are Goddes stewards all, nete of oure owne we bare.

But ah! unhailie pilgrim, lerne of me,   85
Scathe anie give a rentrolle to their Lorde.
Here take my semecope, thou arte bare I see;
Tis thyne; the Seynctes will give me mie rewarde.
He left the pilgrim, and his waie aborde.
Virgynne and hallie Seyncte, who sitte yn gloure,   90
Or give the mittee will, or give the gode man power.

from *The Parlyamente of Sprytes*

Spryte of Segowen speeketh:

Bestoykynge golde was once myne onlie Joie,
Wyth ytte mie Soule wythynne the Coffer laie,
Itte dyd the Mastrie of mie Lyfe emploie,
Bie Nyghte mie Leman and mie Jubbe bie daie –   150

74 *jape* surplice 75 *Limitoure* friar 82 *halline* joy 83 *eathe* ease 85
unhailie unhappy 86 *Scathe* scarce; *rentrolle* reckoning of dues 87 *semecope*
short cloak 89 *aborde* resumed 90 *gloure* glory 91 *mittee* mighty 147
Bestoykynge deceiving 150 *Leman* mistress; *Jubbe* bottle

Once as I dosynge yn the Wytch howre laie,
Thynkeynge howe to benym the Orphyans breadde,
And from the redeless take theyre Goodes awaie,
I from the Skien heard a Voyce whych sayd –
' Thou sleepest but, Loe, Sathan is awake,   155
Some deede thats holie doe or hee thie Soule wylle take.'

I swythyn was upryst wyth feer astounde,
Methoughte yn Merke was plaien Devylles felle :
Strayte did I nomber twentie Aves rounde,
Thoughten full soone for to go to Helle;   160
In the Morne mie Case to a Good Preeste dyd telle,
Who dyd areede mee to ybuild that daie
The Church of Thomas, then to pieces felle.
Mie Hearte dispanded into Heaven laie.

Soone was the Sylver to the Workmenne givne –   165
Twas beste astowde, a Karynte gave to Heaven –
But welle I wote thie Casualles were not soe,
Twas love of Godde that sette thee on the rearynge
Of this fayre Chyrche O Canynge for to doe;
Thys Lymed Buyldynge of so fyne appearynge;   170
Thys Chyrch owre Lesser Buyldyngs all owte-darynge,
Lyke to the Moone wyth Starres of lyttle Lyghte :
And after tymes the feetyve Pyle reverynge,
The Prynce of Chyrches Buylders thee shalle hyghte;
Greet was the Cause but greeter was the effecte :   175
So alle wyll saie who do thys place prospect.

---

152 *benym* steal away   153 *redeless* helpless   157 *swythyn* quickly; *upryst*
arisen   158 *Merke* darkness; *plaien* playing   162 *areede* advise   163 *felle*
fallen   164 *dispanded* expanded   166 *astowde* bestowed; *Karynte* loan;
gave given   167 *Casualles* motives   168 *rearynge* building   170 *Lymed*
noble   173 *feetyve* handsome   174 *hyghte* call

A Knyghte Templar's Spryte speeketh:

In Hallie Lande where Sarasins defyle
The Grounde whereon oure Savyour dyd goe,
And Chryste hys Temple make to Moschyes vyle,
Wordies of Despyte genst oure Savyour throew –   230
There 'twas that wee dyd owre Warfarage doe,
Guardynge the Pylgryms of the Chrystyan faie;
And dyd owre holie Armes in Bloude embrue,
Movynge lyke Thonder Boultes yn drear arraie –
Oure Strokes lyke Levyn tareynge the tall Tree –   235
Oure Godde oure Arme wyth Lethalle Force dyd dree;
Maint Tenures fayre, ande Mannoures of greete Welthe,
Greene Woodes and Brooklettes runnynge throughe the Lee,
Dyd Menne us gyve for theyre deare Soule her Helthe :
Gave Erthlie Ryches for Goodes Hevenlie.   240
Nor dyd we lette oure Ryches untyle bee,
But dyd ybuylde the Temple Chyrche soe fyne,
The whyche ys wroughte abowte so bismarlie,
Itte seemeth Camoys to the wondrynge Eyne.
And ever and anon when Belles rynged,   245
From Place to Place ytte moveth yttes hie heade –
Butte Canynge from the sweate of hys owne browes,
Dyd gette hys Golde and rayse thys fetyve Howse.

Eclogue the Third

Wouldst thou kenn Nature in her better parte?
Goe, serche the Logges and Bordels of the Hynde;

229 *Moschyes* mosques 232 *faie* faith 235 *Levyn* lightning 236 *dree*
drive 237 *Maint* many; *Mannoures* manors 241 *untyle* useless 243
bismarlie curiously 244 *Camoys* crooked upwards 248 *fetyve* beauteous
2 *Logges* huts; *Bordels* cottages; *Hynde* peasant

Gyfe theye have anie itte ys roughemade arte,
Inne hem you see the blakied forme of kynde :
Haveth your minde, a lycheynge of a mynde,   5
Woulde it kenne everich thynge as it mote bee;
Woulde ytte here phrase of th'vulgar from the Hynde,
Wythoute wisegger wordes ande knowlache free,
Gyf soe, rede thys, whych Iche dysportynge pende,
Gif nete besyde, yttes rhyme maie ytte commend :   10

MANNE :

    Botte whether fayre mayde do ye goe,
       O where do ye bend yer waie?
    I wille knowe whether you goe,
       I wylle not be asseled naie.

WOMANNE :

    To Robyn and Nell, all downe in the Delle,   15
       To hele hem at makeynge of Haie.

MANNE :

    Syr Rogerre the Parsone hav hyred mee there,
       Comme, Comme, lette us tryppe ytte awaie;
    We'lle wurche and wylle synge, and wylle drench
         of stronge Beere,
       As longe as the merrie Sommers daie.   20

WOMANNE :

    Howe harde ys mie Dome to Wurch,
       Moke is mie Woe :
    Dame Agnes whoe lies ynne the Chyrche,
       With Birlette golde;
    Wythe gelten aumeres stronge ontolde,   25
       What was shee, moe than me, to be soe?

4 *blaikied* plain 5 *lycheynge* liking 6 *mote* might 7 *vulgar* common
tongue 8 *wisegger* philosopher; *knowlache* wisdom 10 *nete* nought 11
whether whither 14 *asseled* answered 16 *hele* help 19 *wurche* work;
drench drink 21 *Dome* fate 22 *Moke* much 24 *Birlette* hood 25 *gelten*
aumeres cloth-of-gold mantles

MANNE :

> I kenne Syr Roger from afar,
> Tryppynge over the'Lea,
> Ich ask whie the Loverds Son
> Is moe than mee.   30

SYR ROGER :

The sweltrie Sonne dothe hie apace hys Wayne.
From everich beme, a seme of lyfe doe falle;
Swythyn scille oppe the haie uponne the Playne,
Methynckes the Cocks begynneth to gre talle :
Thys ys alyche oure Doome, the great, the smalle,   35
Moste withe and be forwynd by Deathis darte;
See the swote flourette hathe noe swote at alle;
Itte wythe the ranke wede berethe evalle parte,
The Cravent, Warriour, and the Wyse be blent :
Alyche to drie awaie, with those theie did bemente.   40

MANNE :

> All-a-Boon Syr Priest, all-a-boon,
> Bye yer Preesteschype nowe saye unto mee :
> Sir Gaufryd the Knyghte, who lyveth harde bie,
> Whie should hee, than me
> Bee moe greate,   45
> Inne honnoure, Knyghtehoode and Estate?

SYR ROGERRE :

Attourne thine Eyne arounde thys haied mee,
Tentyflie loke arounde the chaper dell;
An answer to thie Barganette here see,
Thys welked flouertte wylle a Leson telle :   50

30 *moe* greater   31 *sweltrie* sultry; *hie* drive   32 *seme* seed   33 *swythyn*
quickly; *scille* gather   34 *gre* grow   36 *withe* wither; *forwynd* dried up
37 *swote* sweet   38 *evalle* equal   39 *Cravent* coward; *blent* passed away
40 *bemente* lament   41 *All-a-boon* If you please   47 *haied mee* hay-covered
field   48 *Tentyflie* carefully; *chaper* parched   49 *Barganette* song   50
welked withered

Arist, it blew, itte florished, and dyd welle,
Lokeynge ascaunce upon the neighboure greene,

Yet with the deigned greene, yttes rennome felle,
Eftsonnes ytte shronke upon the daie-brente Playne.
Didde not yttes loke, whilest ytte there dyd stonde,   55
To croppe ytte in the bodde, move somme drede honde.

Sycke ys the Waie of Lyffe : the Loverds Ente,
Mooveth the Robber hym therfor to slea :
Gyf thou has ethe, the Shadowe of Contente,
Believe the Trothe, theeres none moe haile yan thee :   60
Thou wurchest; welle, canne thatte, a trobble bee,
Slothe moe wulde jade thee, than the roughest daie,
Couldest thou the Kivercled of Soughlys see,
Thou wuldst eftsoones see Trothe, Inne whatte I saie;
Botte lette mee heere thie waie offe Lyffe; and thanne   65
Heare thou from mee the Lyffs of odher menne.

MANNE :

            I ryse wythe the Sonne,
            Lyche hym to dryve the Wayne
            And eere mie Wurche is don
            I synge a Songe or twane.   70
            I followe the plough tayle,
            Wythe a long jubb of Ale –
            Botte of the Maydens – oh,
            Itte lacketh notte to telle;
            Syr Preeste mote notte crie woe,   75
            Culde hys Bull do as welle –
            I daunce the beste Heie deygnes,

51 *Arist* (having) arisen   53 *deigned* disdained; *rennome* glory   54 *daie-
brente* sun-parched   56 *bodde* bud   57 *Sycke* such; *Loverds* lord's; *Ente*
purse   59 *ethe* ease   60 *haile* happy; *yan* than   63 *Kivercled* hidden part;
Soughlys souls   72 *jubb* bottle   77 *Heie deygnes* country dance

81

And foile the wysest feygnes.
On everych Seynctes hie daie,
Wythe the mynstrelle am I seen,   80
All a footeynge it awaie,
Wythe Maydens on the Greene –
But oh – I wyshe to be moe great,
In rennome Tenure and Estate.

SYR ROGERRE :
Has thou ne sene a Tree uponne a Hylle,   85
Whose unliste braunces rechen far toe syghte;
Whan fuired Unwers doe the Heaven fylle,
Itte shaketh deere yn dole and moke affryghte :
Whilst the Congeon flowr'tte abessie dyghte,
Stondeth unhurte, unquaced bie the Storme;   90
Syke is a Picte of Lyffe : the manne of myghte,
Is tempest-chaft : hys woe great as hys forme –
Thie self a flourette of a small accounte,
Wouldst harder felle the Wynde, as hygher thee dydste mount.

The Worlde

Fadre. Sonne. Mynstrelles.

FADRE :
To the Worlde newe ande ytts bestoykeynge Waies,
Thys Coistrelle Sonne of myne ys all mie Care;
Ye mynstrelles, warne hymme how wyth rede he straies
Where guiled Vyce dothe spredde her mascilde Snare.

78 *feygnes* feints (in fighting) 86 *unliste* unbounded 87 *fuired Unwers*
furious tempests 88 *deere* dire; *dole* terror; *affryghte* terrifies 89
Congeon dwarf; *abessie* humbly; *dyghte* decked 90 *unquaced* unharmed
91 *Picte* picture 94 *felle* feel. *Fadre* father 1 *bestoykeynge* deceitful
2 *Coistrelle* young 3 *rede* counsel 4 *guiled* guileful; *mascilde* meshed

82

To gettynge Wealthe I woulde he shoulde be bredde   5
And Couronnes of rudde Goulde, ne Glorie, round hys Head.

1st Mynstrelle :
Mie Name is Intereste – tis I
Dothe ynto alle Boosoms flie;
Echone hylten secrets myne,
None so wordie good and dygne   10
Botte wylle fynde it to theyre Coaste,
Intereste wylle rule the roaste.
I to everichone gyve lawes :
Selfe ys fyrst yn everich cause.

2nd Mynstrelle :
I amm a faytoure flame   15
Of lemmies melancholi,
Love somme behyghte mie name,
Some doe anemp me follie;
Inne sprytes of meltynge molde
I sette mie burneynge sele,   20
To mee a goulers goulde
Doeth nete a pyne avele,
I pre upon the helthe;
And from Gode redeynge flee,
The manne who woulde gette wealthe   25
Must never thynke of mee.

3rd Mynstrelle :
I bee the Queede of Pryde, mie spyrynge heade
Mote reche the cloudes and style be rysynge hie,
Too lyttle is the earthe to bee mie bedde,
Too hannow for mie breetheynge place the skie;   30

9 *hylten* hides 11 *Coaste* cost 15 *faytoure* deceitful 16 *lemmies* gleams
17 *behyghte* call 18 *anemp* name 21 *goulers* miser's 22 *pyne* pin 24
Gode redeynge good advice 27 *Queede* devil; *spyrynge* towering 30
hannow narrow

Daynous I see the worlde bineth me lie
Botte to mie betterres, I soe lyttle gree.
Aneuthe a shadow of a shade I bee,
Tys to the smalle alleyn that I canne multyplie.

4TH MYNSTRELLE :
I am the Queed of goulers, looke arounde :   35
The ayres aboute mee thieves doe represente,
Bloudsteyned robbers sprynge from oute the grounde,
And airie vysons swarme around mie ente;
O save mie monies, ytte ys theyre entente
To nymme the redde Godde of mie fremded sprighte   40
Whatte joie canne goulers have or daie or nyghte?

5TH MYNSTRELLE :
Vice bee I hyghte : onne golde fulle ofte I ryde,
Fulle fayre unto the syghte for aie I seeme;
Mie ugsomness wythe goldenne veyles I hyde,
Laieynge mie lovers ynne a sylkenne dreme;   45
Botte whan mie untrue pleasaunce have byn tryde,
Thanne doe I showe alle horrownesse and row,
And those I have ynne nette woulde feyne mie grype eschew.

6TH MYNSTRELLE :
I bee greete Dethe, all ken mee bie the name,
Botte none can saie howe I doe loose the spryghte;   50
Goode menne mie tardyinge delaie doethe blame,
Botte moste ryche goulerres from me take a flyghte;
Myckle of wealthe I see whereere I came,
Doethe mie ghastness mockle multyplye
Ande maketh hem afrayde to lyve or dye.   55

31 *Daynous* disdainful 32 *gree* grow 33 *Aneuthe* less than 34 *alleyn*
alone 35 *Queed* devil 38 *ente* purse 40 *nymme* steal; *fremded* frightened
41 *goulers* misers 44 *ugsomness* ugliness 47 *horrownesse* beastliness; *row*
horror 52 *goulerres* misers

FADRE :
Howe, villeyn Mynstrelles, and is this your rede?
Awaie, awaie : I wyll ne geve a curse.
Mie sonne, mie sonne, of this mie speeche take hede,
Nothynge ys goode thatte bryngeth not to purse.

'There was a Broder of Orderys Blacke'

There was a Broder of Orderys Blacke
  In mynster of Brystowe Cittie :
He layd a Damoisell onne her Backe
  So guess yee the Taile of mie Dittie.

'Theere was a Broder of Orderys Whyte'

Theere was a Broder of Orderys Whyte,
Hee songe hys Masses yn the Nyghte,
  Ave Maria Jesus Maria;
The nonnes al slepeynge yn the Dortoure
Thoughte hym of al syngeynge Freeres the Floure,   5
  Ave Maria, Jesu Maria.

Suster Agnes looved his syngeyng welle,
And songe with hem too the sothen to telle,
  Ave Maria, Jesus Maria;
But be ytte ne sed bie Elde or yynge   10

56 *rede* advice   4 *Dortoure* dormintory   9 *sothen* truth   10 *yynge* young

That ever dheye oderwyse dyd synge
  Than Ave Maria, Jesu Maria.

This Broder was called everich wheere,
To Kenshamm and to Brystol Nonnere,
  Ave Maria, Jesus Maria;   15
Botte seyynge of Masses dyd wurch hym so lowe
Above hys Skynne hys Bonys did growe,
  Ave Maria, Jesu Maria.

He eaten Beefe ande Dyshes of Mows
And hontend everych Knyghtys House,   20
  With Ave Maria, Jesus Maria;
And beynge ance moe in gode lyken,
He songe to the Nonnes and was poren agan,
  With Ave Maria, Jesu Maria.

The Gouler's Requiem

(quasi Requiem) by Canynge

Mie boolie Entes, adiewe : ne more the Syghte
Of guilden Merke shalle mete mie joieous Eyne;
Ne moe the sylver Noble sheenynge bryghte,
Shalle fylle mie hande wythe weighte to speke ytte fyne;
Ne moe : Ne moe : alas, I calle you myne;   5
Whyder must you? – ah, whydher moste I goe?
I kenne not either! Oh mie Emmers dygne,
To parte wythe you wyll wurche me myckle Woe.

14 *nonnere* nunnery 19 *Mows* porridge 20 *hontend* haunted 22 *ance moe* once more; *lyken* health. *Gouler* miser 1 *boolie* beloved; *Entes* coffers 2 *Merke* marks 7 *Emmers dygne* worthy comforters

I must begon, butte where I dare nott telle,
O Storth unto mie Mynde, I fere to Helle!   10

Soone as the Morne dyd dyghte the roddie Sonne,
A Shade of Theves eache streacke of Lyghte dyd seme;
Whan yn the Heaven full half hys Course was ronne,
Eche styrrynge Nayghboure dyd mie harte enfleme;
Thie Losse, or quyck or slepe, was aie mie dreme,   15
For thee, O goulde! I did the Lawe ycrase,
For thee I gottenne, or bie Wiles or breme;
Inn thee I all mie Joie and goode dyd wase;
Botte nowe to mee thie pleasaunce ys ne moe,
I kenne not but for thee, I to the Qwood muste goe.   20

Onn Johne a Dalbenie

Johne makes a Jarre 'boute Lancaster and yorke :
Bee stille gode manne, and learne to mynde thie worke.

10 *Storth* death   11 *dyghte* deck   14 *enfleme* alarm   15 *quyck* awake   16
ycrase break   17 *breme* force   18 *wase* waste   20 *Qwood* Devil

Notes

ACKNOWLEDGED POEMS

Apostate Will　　Manuscript dated *April 14th 1764*, i.e. when Chatterton was twelve years old.

1–2 Bristol had been a centre of Methodism since 1793 when John Wesley founded his first chapel there. Charges of avarice and hypocrisy were frequently made against the Methodists, as against other dissenters.

17 *Bingham, Young and Stillingfleet:* Ecclesiastical historians and partisans of the Church of England.

To Horace Walpole　　Probably written at the end of Chatterton's correspondence with Walpole, in July 1769. Despite the note in Chatterton's hand at the foot of the page, the poem appears to be unfinished.

Journal 6th　　A verse letter to John Baker, a friend of Chatterton's who had emigrated to Charleston, South Carolina. The Journal consists of several sections on different subjects, from which I have selected one complete section (lines 173–254 in Taylor's edition). I number the lines from 1 to 82 because the section is in effect a complete poem, apart from a transitional passage following my line 82 (Taylor's 254) which leads into a satirical ode.

The title is quite arbitrary: the copy in the British Museum is folded so that part of a note at the end of the manuscript, ' *Journal 6th*, Ended Sat : Even 30 Sept 1769–' appears as the title. *Journal 6th* may mean that it was begun on September 6th, or it may have been one of a numbered series of which the rest is now lost.

35–6 Possibly a play on the sense of *rake* as a gardening-implement.

57–8 Skeat primly omits these lines.

232 i.e., 'Really an animal *except* in hoofs and hide'.

Elegy to Phillips   Written November 1769. This text is from the first of two versions of the poem.

Thomas Phillips, Chatterton's schoolfriend, died at Fairford on November 1, 1769. Elegiac convention and personal affection permit Chatterton to exaggerate his friend's gifts as a poet.

7 *corded shell* The lyre. One of Chatterton's favourite periphrases.

53 Compare Keats, *Ode to Autumn*, 24.

101–4 A note in Chatterton's hand reads 'Expunged as too flowry for Grief'.

103 Compare Gray, *Elegy Wrote in a Country Churchyard*, 2.

The Defence   Dated 25 December 1769. The poet is apparently defending himself against charges of impiety.

1 *Smith* Richard Smith, friend and contemporary of Chatterton.

5 *Shears* A minor Bristol satirist. Chatterton seems to be suggesting that Shears lacks the intelligence to achieve either fame or infamy. Cropping of the ears was a common penalty for sedition.

7 *Lawrence* Either Herbert Lawrence, surgeon and minor author or Thomas Lawrence, Bristol innkeeper and father of the painter of the same name.

9 *Taylor* Apparently a clergyman and disciple of the Reverend Alexander Catcott.

Alexander Catcott was the brother of George Catcott, the pewterer. A clergyman, he published in 1761 a *Treatise on the Deluge,* attempting to reconcile the findings of geology with the book of Genesis. His theories amused Chatterton.

34 *Whitfield* George Whitfield, a Methodist who adhered sternly to the doctrine of predestination.

Penny Devout minor poet of Bristol, author of *An Incentive to the Love of God* (1769).

Bacchanalian   Written in 1770. A song from *The Revenge,* Chatterton's two-act 'Burletta'.

To Miss Hoyland   Written early in 1770. Eleanor Hoyland was a Bristol girl to whom Chatterton wrote several poems on behalf of his friend John Baker, who had emigrated to South Carolina. The purpose of the poems is not clear, since Baker wrote that 'I have entirely forgot that celebrated beauty that gave me so much pleasing uneasiness at Bristol.'

11 *Camplin* John Camplin, precentor of Bristol Cathedral.

13 *Catcott* See note to *The Defence*, 9.

February: An Elegy   Written in 1770. Published in the *Town and Country Magazine* February 1770. Compare, *passim,* Swift's *Description of the Morning* and Gay's *Trivia.*

9 *Goat* Capricorn   *Waterer* Aquarius.

60 *Gouts*   Gushes (of water); or the disease gout.

69 Johnson's politics were opposed to Chatterton's, the latter being a supporter of Wilkes. Johnson had lived, until his death in 1784, on a pension from Bute, another of Chatterton's *bêtes-noire.*

The Art of Puffing   Dated July 22 1770.

Puffing Advertising and generally pushing the sales of a book.

5 *Curl* Edmund Curl (1765–1747) a bookseller and publisher whose unscrupulous practices were almost proverbial.

9 *Pottinger* Probably James Pottinger, a successful hack author.

10 *Cooke* It is not clear to which of many Cook(e)s Chatterton refers.

13 *Baldwin* Unknown.

14 *Cuts* Illustrations; *hums* tricks or hoaxes.

16 Paoli was a leader of the fight for Corsican independence and James Boswell was a supporter of his cause. Paoli visited London at this time, amid much publicity.

19 Oliver Goldsmith (1730–1774) whose *Deserted Village* had just appeared.

22 *Bingley* William Bingley, publisher of Wilkes's journal *The North Briton;* recently imprisoned for sedition. The reference here is obscure.

24 *Edmunds* The editor of the *Middlesex Journal,* imprisoned in

1770 for political offences.

37 *Flexney* William Flexney, bookseller and publisher of Churchill's satires.

On the Immortality of the Soul The date of composition is uncertain. The poem was written as an 'impromptu' in the presence of Chatterton's friend William Smith, before the poet's departure for London.

2 *Mystery* Precisely what mystery this is, is not clear.

ROWLEY POEMS

Ælla Probably written in 1769. The action and characters are fictitious. The play is written almost entirely in the ten-line stanzas, ending in an alexandrine, which Chatterton seems to have adapted from Spenser.

Personnes Represented Chatterton imagines an amateur performance. The cast includes several of his favourite imaginary medieval Bristolians.

105 *cherisaunei* Chatterton takes over a misprint from Bailey's Dictionary, which glosses *cherisaunie* as comfort, and adds a further error of his own. The historical form is *cherisaunce*.

209 *bestoikerre* from Bailey, who misreads *beswike* (betray) as *bestoike*.

233 *alatche* Apparently invented by Chatterton.

272 Celmonde's comment is understandable but tactless.

281 *nesh* (delicate) is still current in north country dialects.

312 *tere* 'This is a most astonishing blunder. Bailey gives "*Teres major*, a round smooth *muscle* of the arm, &c." Hence Chatterton makes *teres* equivalent to muscles, and then deduces a singular form *tere* !' (Skeat) *Health* is Chatterton's own gloss.

369 *gaberdine* 'A loose, coarse frock, more fit for a monster like Caliban than for a warrior' (Skeat).

373 *slughornes* From an old spelling of modern *slogan*. Chatterton, who knew only that the sound of 'slughornes' normally accompanied fighting, assumed that it was a kind of trumpet.

515 *aumere* Bailey glosses as 'a welt, skirt, or border' and Chatterton follows. In fact it means a purse.

536ff. Compare *I Henry IV* v.i.135ff.

578 'This line is, . . . in all probability, a riddle without an answer, and was intended to be so.' (Skeat)

965ff. I give the refrain in full rather than disfigure the text with '&c's'.

968 Compare *Hamlet* iv.v.192–5.

982– Compare Shelley, *Ghasta,* 1–4.

1165 *deslavatie* 'This absurd word is made up from Bailey's "*deslavy,* lecherous, beastly," which he wrongly fathers upon Chaucer'. (Skeat)

1363 *carns* Rewriting the word as *stones,* the irritable Skeat comments, 'Chatterton has "A pile of carns", not being aware, it would appear, that a cairn is *the pile itself.'*

An Excelente Balade of Charitie   Submitted to the *Town and Country Magazine,* on July 4 1770, but not published. The influence of Chaucer is clearly apparent in the description of the Abbott; and the basic theme is, of course, that of the Good Samaritan. Early critics praised especially Chatterton's portrayal of the gathering storm, and the poem is generally regarded as his best work.

75 a *Limitour* was a licensed begging friar who worked over a limited area. Chatterton borrowed the idea and the word from Chaucer.

The Parlyamente of Sprytes   Written late in 1768. The poem is a pageant, supposedly written by Rowley, to honour Canynge, builder of the Church of St. Mary Redcliff, on the occasion of its consecration. A procession of famous church- and temple-builders appears in spirit to praise Canynge's work, and the probity of his motives. I select two of the best speeches.

Segowen A note by the poet describes him as 'An Usurer a Native of Lombardy'. He is fictitious.

Eclogue the Third Probably written in 1769.

2 *bordels* Here and elsewhere Chatterton uses the word to mean 'cottages'. In fact it means 'brothels'. How the mistake arose it is hard to see, since Chatterton elsewhere uses *bordelier* correctly, to mean 'a frequenter of brothels'.

16 Medieval priests were addressed as 'Sir'.

The Worlde   Probably written early in 1769. Chatterton is by implication defending his own growing dislike of the business world. The canny father's attitude to the 'World' is ambivalent: on the one hand he deplores its vices, on the other he wants his son to amass riches rather than 'Glorie'. The minstrels who play Interest, Love, Pride, Usury, Vice and Death are a little too candid and reveal the true implications of the father's attitude, leaving him discomfited but still feebly asserting that profit is the only good.

57 *Curse*: '*Kerse* is old English for *cress*; hence, "not worth a *kerse*" meant, originally, "not worth a *cress*". It is very improbable, however, that Chatterton knew this. In the last line, he at last deigns to call a purse, a purse; having so often called it an *ente*.' (Skeat)

'*There Was a Broder of Orderys Blacke*'   Date uncertain.

'*There Was a Broder of Orderys Whyte*'   Date uncertain.

The Gouler's Requiem   Probably written in May 1769. It is not clear why the poem should be attributed to Canynge rather than to Rowley.

quasi Requiem 'a false requiem'.

4 Taylor justly praises the 'startingly emphatic' vividness of this line, as of lines 6 and 12.

Onn Johne a Dalbenie   Written late in 1768 or early in 1769.

Appendix A

'Chatterton's Last Verses'

Farewell, Bristolia's dingy piles of brick,
Lovers of Mammon, worshippers of Trick!
Ye spurn'd the boy who gave you antique lays,
And paid for learning with your empty praise.
Farewell, ye guzzling aldermanic fools,
By nature fitted for Corruption's tools!
I go to where celestial anthems swell;
But you, when you depart, will sink to Hell.
Farewell, my Mother! Cease, my anguish'd soul,
Nor let Distraction's billows o'er me roll!
Have mercy, Heaven! when here I cease to live,
And this last act of wretchedness forgive.

T.C.

August 24, 1770

Appendix B

Chatterton's Will

All this wrote between 11 and 2 o'clock Saturday, in the utmost distress of mind. April 14, 1770.

This is the last Will and Testament of me, Thomas Chatterton, of the city of Bristol; being sound in body, or it is the fault of my last surgeon : the soundness of my mind, the coroner and jury are to be the judges of, desiring them to take notice, that the most perfect masters of human nature in Bristol distinguish me by the title of the Mad Genius; therefore, if I do a mad action, it is conformable to every action of my life, which all savoured of insanity.

Item. If after my death, which will happen tomorrow night before eight o'clock, being the Feast of the Resurrection, the coroner and jury bring it in lunacy, I will and direct, that Paul Farr, Esq. and Mr. John Flower, at their joint expense, cause my body to be interred in the tomb of my fathers, and raise the monument over me to the height of four feet five inches, placing the present flat stone on the top, and adding six tablets.

Item. I give all my vigour and fire of youth to Mr. George Catcott, being sensible he is most in want of it.

Item. From the same charitable motive, I give and bequeath unto the Reverend Mr. Camplin senior, all my humility. To Mr. Burgum all my prosody and grammar, – likewise one moiety of my modesty; the other to any young lady who can prove without blushing that she wants that valuable commodity. To Bristol, all my spirit and disinterestedness; parcels of goods unknown on her quay since the days of Canning and Rowley! 'Tis true, a charitable gentleman, one Mr. Colston, smuggled a considerable quantity of it, but it being proved that he was a papist, the Worshipful Society of Aldermen endeavoured to throttle him with the Oath of Allegiance. I leave also my religion to Dr. Cutts Barton, Dean of Bristol, hereby empowering the sub-sacrist to strike him on the head when he goes to sleep in church. My powers of utterance I give to the Reverend Mr. Broughton, hoping he will employ them to a better purpose than reading lectures on the immortality of the soul. I leave the Reverend Mr. Catcott some little of my free-thinking, that he may put on spectacles of Reason, and see how vilely he is duped in believing the Scriptures literally. I wish he and his brother George would know how far I am their real enemy; but I have an unlucky way of raillery,

95

and when the strong fit of satire is upon me, I spare neither friend nor foe. This is my excuse for what I have said of them elsewhere. I leave Mr. Clayfield the sincerest thanks my gratitude can give; and I will and direct that, whatever any person may think the pleasure of reading my works worth, they immediately pay their own valuation to him, since it is then become a lawful debt to me, and to him as my executor in this case.

I leave my moderation to the politicians on both sides of the question. I leave my generosity to our present Right Worshipful Mayor, Thomas Harris, Esq. I give my abstinence to the company at the Sheriff's annual feast in general, more particularly the Aldermen.

Item. I give and bequeath to Mr. Matthew Mease a mourning ring with this motto, 'Alas, poor Chatterton!' provided he pays for it himself. Item. I leave the young ladies all the letters they have had from me, assuring them that they need be under no apprehensions from the appearance of my ghost, for I die for none of them. – Item. I leave all my debts, the whole not five pounds, to the payment of the charitable and generous Chamber of Bristol, on penalty, if refused, to hinder every member from a good dinner by appearing in the form of a bailiff. If in defiance of this terrible spectre, they obstinately persist in refusing to discharge my debts, let my two creditors apply to the supporters of the Bill of Rights. – Item. I leave my mother and sister to the protection of my friends, if I have any.

Executed in the presence of Omniscience this 14th of April, 1770.

Thos. Chatterton.